with love,

Understanding Rett Syndrome:

A Practical Guide for Parents, Teachers, and Therapists

Understanding Rett Syndrome:

A Practical Guide for Parents, Teachers, and Therapists

Barbro Lindberg

Stockholm Institute of Education
Department of Educational Research

Foreword by Prof. Dr. Andreas Rett, Vienna

Published under the editorial supervision of
Ludwig Boltzmann Institute for Research on
Brain Damage in Children,
Vienna, Austria

Hogrefe & Huber Publishers
Toronto • Lewiston, NY • Bern • Göttingen • Stuttgart

Library of Congress Cataloging-in-Publication Data
Lindberg, Barbro.
    Understanding Rett Syndrome : a practical guide for parents,
teachers, therapists / by Barbro Lindberg ; preface by Andreas
Rett.
    p. cm.
    Includes bibliographical references.
    ISBN 0-88937-033-8 : $22.50
    1. Rett syndrome — Popular works. 2. Rett syndrome — Patients-
- Education. I. Title
RJ506.R47L56 1991
618.92'8 — DC20   90-34409
                                                                CIP

Canadian Cataloguing in Publication Data
Lindberg, Barbro
    Understanding Rett Syndrome

Translation of: Rett syndrom.
Includes bibliographical references.
ISBN 0-88937-033-8

1. Rett syndrome. 2. Rett syndrome - Patients - Care.
3. Rett syndrome - Patients - Education.
I. Title.

RJ506.R47L56 1991   618.92'8588   C90-093863-3

**Retts Syndrom — en kartläggning av
psykologiska och pedagogiska erfarenheter i Sverige**
First published in Swedish by Stockholm Institute of Education Press, 1988.

12 Bruce Park Avenue   P.O. Box 51
Toronto, ON   M4P 2S3   Lewiston, NY 14082
CANADA   USA

Printed in USA
ISBN 0-88937-033-8
Hogrefe & Huber Publishers, Toronto • Lewiston, NY • Bern • Göttingen • Stuttgart
ISBN 3-456-81868-8
Hogrefe & Huber Publishers, Bern • Stuttgart • Toronto • Lewiston, NY

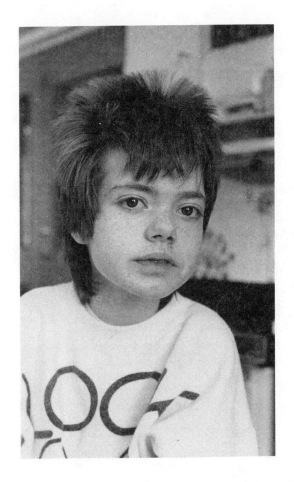

With my thanks to Ulrika and to all the other girls.

ACKNOWLEDGEMENTS

This study was supported by grants from:

The Allmänna Barnhus Foundation,
The Claes Groschinsky Memorial Foundation,
The Folke Bernadotte Foundation,
The Frimurare Barnhus Foundation,
The Norrbacka-Eugenia Foundation,
The Sven Jerring Foundation, and
The Sävstaholm Foundation.

TABLE OF CONTENTS

Communication
Emotional Channels
Large Fluctuations in Behavior
Emotional Reactions
Insecure Identity

FOREWORD

Rett Syndrome: A Survey of Psychological and Educational Experiences in Sweden

In this volume, with great devotion and impact, Barbro Lindberg presents the clinical picture and treatment modalities of Rett syndrome. The disorder was first described more than 30 years ago. However, only through the incredible activities undertaken by Kathy Hunter in the United States has it received such unusually widespread international attention.

Described here is a clinical syndrome that has now been diagnosed in more than 31 countries, and the extent to which the picture is everywhere consistent, is nothing less than remarkable . This is a disorder found exclusively in girls, presenting a particular characterization of neurological symptoms. Today research is being conducted worldwide in search of its cause.

Barbro Lindberg's special involvement has been in the day-to-day life of these girls and women. Having studied roles of their parents and guardians, she presents her data and discussion with painstaking exactness and detail.

This monograph affords a very empathetic view of the situation these parents are in and will certainly be a help in enabling coping with such a difficult chronic situation that concerns not just the mother, but the entire family.

I hope this book will be widely disseminated. The reader should note that it offers valuable help with regard to the social, physical, and ethical aspects of dealing with a most difficult congenital disorder.

Andreas Rett, M. D.

PREFACE

This report was written to be the book I would have liked to have had, when a girl with Rett syndrome was placed in my class at a time when I had no knowledge or experience of the disorder. This student of mine, and my feeling of inadequacy for her, incited me to find out more about the syndrome. I realized that I had to really understand her acting, in order to understand how to act myself.

This book is primarily intended for people close to those with Rett syndrome; parents and professionals who are trying to make everyday life easier and better for them. It is based on a study of Swedish females, but the conclusions are general and valid to all those with classical Rett syndrome, and so I hope that this English version will find many new readers, and that it will provide an answer to some of the questions you may have.

I want to thank Professor Andres Rett for his generosity and interest in the translation of the book, and Dr. Mary Murphy, members of the IRSA, and many good friends who helped me with the translation, correcting me and making the language more enjoyable. And my special thanks to Kathy Hunter, for all her support and understanding.

Barbro Lindberg

INTRODUCTION

1 Background

Rett syndrome is a very specific disorder which affects girls only. It cannot yet be demonstrated by any medical test, but has to be diagnosed from each particular case history and total clinical picture.

These children are born "healthy" and their psychomotor development is apparently normal up to 6-18 months of age. Then comes a devastating period of slowing down or stagnation, followed by regression.

The onset of the illness can be either insidious and gradual or quite sudden and dramatic. The girls may scream or cry inconsolably. They may, without any apparent reason, withdraw from the outer world into a state of isolation or exhibit behaviors which may lead to the misdiagnosis of autism during this stage of the disorder. However, in the course of time, the children improve in social contacts, and a number of other specific symptoms appear which make it possible to make a more precise diagnosis. Girls and women with Rett syndrome are mentally retarded, have severe gross and fine motor handicaps, epileptic seizures, some remaining autistic-like features, communication disabilities, various kinds of stereotypic behaviors, and often gastrointestinal disturbances (such as vomiting, constipation, and abnormal abdominal distension).

The onset of the disorder and rapidity of its progress varies with each case, as does the intensity of the different symptoms. However, all the girls will be severely impeded in their development by the progressive nature of the syndrome. In time, the gross motor deterioration will increase, although the disorder as a whole is not characterized by a continuous downward trend, but rather by periods of impairment and deterioration, alternating with periods of improvement or stability. Up to now there are no grounds for believing that the illness will lead to premature death. On the contrary, despite their severe handicaps, many of the girls will live well into adulthood, and there are some women over 50 years old diagnosed with Rett syndrome. However, with increasing age it is more difficult to make the diagnosis, as the clinical picture becomes less easily differentiated from other severe brain disorders.

This syndrome is not new, but knowledge of it has only recently become more widespread. Before they met in the early 1980s, Professor Andreas Rett, of Vienna, after whom the disorder is named, and Professor Bengt Hagberg, in Gothenburg, Sweden, had both independently observed and collected data on a number of girls with the condition. Since 1983, when data concerning this hitherto unknown syndrome and its manifestations were presented in an American neurology journal, interest in the disorder has increased explosively, and new cases are continuously being reported as the awareness of the clinical picture grows. Today, the disorder can be found all over the world and its incidence is believed to be 1/10,000 female births. This implies that in girls it is three times as common as phenylketonuria (PKU), a congenital error of metabolism which can be diagnosed by testing of the blood of the newborn.

In the autumn of 1986 there were approximately 1,150 reported cases of Rett syndrome in the world. In Sweden at that time there were about 80, the youngest being 2 years old and the oldest over 40.

The cause of Rett syndrome is so far unknown. Today, it is believed that it results from some congenital biochemical error in the metabolism of the central nervous system. The fact that the syndrome occurs only in girls indicates that genetic factors related to the x-chromosome may be involved, but there is as yet no complete theory of the underlying mechanisms. Despite the assumption of a genetic basis for the disease, the risk of familial recurrence is considered to be very small, less than one percent.

All over the world intense research into the cause of Rett syndrome is going on. How the disorder may be prevented remains unknown, however, and for the girls already afflicted there is, as yet, no established medical cure.

Physicians cannot yet give very much help to these girls. Therefore their parents, physical therapists, and personnel in schools and daycare centers must work together with physicians in a common effort to make a difficult situation more tolerable.

2 My Own Background and Personal Inducements

I have worked for 12 years as a teacher of severely multihandicapped children and for many years I had a child with Rett syndrome in my class.

This particular girl caused many questions to be raised when the effects of the disorder and the intentions of the training bumped into each other. How, for instance, should behaviors resulting not from lack of stimulation but from damaged brain function be handled? Is it beneficial to interfere with the hand stereotypies? Is it possible to eliminate them? Maybe it is better to find ways to use the stereotypies in a constructive manner? But then maybe they will be reinforced — and can that really be beneficial?

Working with multihandicapped children means that everything takes time, a long time. The multihandicapped child needs an unlimited amount of patience, and is dependent on the help of others in order to eat and go to the bathroom, dress and undress, regulate body temperature, change positions and move, get her wishes, needs, and feelings truly interpreted and satisfied, and even understand what is going to happen the next minute.

For those working with the child, it is a question of trying to develop and train her as much as possible, based on her individual needs and motivation. It is much more pleasant, for instance, to work with physical and mental training at the same time. But often this is not possible, and one feels that the time available is not sufficient to meet all the needs of the child. Of course when there is not time enough for everything, one has to give priority to something. It may seem that nothing can be more important than enticing an emotionally and socially withdrawn child to come out of its isolation — and so maybe one would like to concentrate on that and ignore physical therapy, which may be painful and incomprehensible to the child. But perhaps in the long run it will be still more painful for the child to live with a stiff and distorted body and all the resulting consequences. How motivated will that child be to live in joyful relations with the outer world?

There are always questions, but the answers are more difficult to find. The students are totally dependent on the knowledge and devotion of the staff — and on the financial means available.

I used trial and error with my student. I thought we were doing well — but perhaps we could have done better. I contacted Professor Hagberg and received from him a continuous flow of information about research on the disorder and its medical consequences. This was of great value in helping me to understand better what was part of the clinical picture and what was part of my student "herself."

Through Professor Hagberg I also got in touch with other children with Rett syndrome and the people close to them. I found that we had many thoughts in common. It seemed more and more justified to gather additional data about this population in order to learn what is important to them and how to work in a good educational/therapeutic way. When I learned that a medical survey of girls and women with Rett syndrome in Sweden was going to start, I decided to try to undertake a parallel psychological/educational survey.

＊ My project has been associated with The Handicap Research Group at the Stockholm Institute of Education and was under the supervision of Britta Alin-Åkerman. The project was completed in parallel with the medical project, "Rett Syndrome in Sweden. Neurodevelopment, Nosology, Pathophysiology" performed by Dr. Ingegerd Witt-Engerström under the supervision of Professor Bengt Hagberg. They have both given me the medical facts and enhanced my picture of these females.

3 Aim

The aim of my study has been to gain a more extensive and varied picture of what Rett syndrome really means to the individuals affected — what the handicaps are in all respects, what emotional, social, and mental abilities are present, what the girls' strong points are, and what difficulties require special attention. I also wanted to get some idea of how parents and staff have tried to help these girls through teaching and therapy. There were no records of this work, but I considered the state of knowledge in Sweden to be quite extensive and well worth documenting in this way.

My aim has not been to say what is "best" for the girls or what "should" be done. Instead, I hope that this report will contribute to a wider and more profound understanding of these girls in order to form a basis for those working with individuals with Rett syndrome to feel more sure and creative in seeking to solve their problems.

4 Sample

When I started my survey, my plan was to meet all the girls in Sweden with Rett syndrome, but new cases were found at a rate not anticipated. Thus, I had no choice but to impose a time limit on the survey and include only those cases that I had contacted before my deadline.

As a result, the sample consists of 39 females from 2 to 29 years old. They have been divided into age groups: 2-6 years (7), 7-11 years (13), 12-16 years (8), 17-21 years (7), 22-29 years (4). These individuals represent different stages in the course of the disorder and include those who are very severely afflicted as well as those more mildly affected. The group age 2-16 years includes all but three of the cases reported up to June, 1986 (that is 28 of 31). In the group age 16-29 years, my sample includes 11 of the 27 cases reported up to June 1986. Since this age group is more homogeneous than the younger one, I considered it important to give preference to a more complete sample of the younger girls. I have also met five girls who were later diagnosed as atypical or "formes frustes;" that is, they do not show all the symptoms necessary for a diagnosis or their psychomotor development is somewhat different from that of those girls with classical Rett syndrome. Furthermore, I have also met a couple of individuals where the diagnosis has been uncertain and has later been altered to a different one. Only individuals with classical Rett syndrome are included in the report, although all the girls have contributed by elucidating the syndrome and setting bounds for it.

5 Methods

The methods used were observations and interviews. These were undertaken by myself from the autumn of 1985 to the autumn of 1986. Each girl was observed both in her home setting and in school (daycare center/day center) for 1-2 days. I made continuous observations, and in some cases the observations were supplemented by films and videos (when available).

The observations were made in situations and during activities that occurred independently of my visit. During each observation session I tried to gather information on as many as possible of the questions that were of interest to me, but the circumstances were not sufficiently uniform to make the observations of the different girls directly comparable.

Systematic interviews using a large number of questions were performed, where members of the family, school personnel, and others helping to take care of the girls told of their experiences. In most cases the interviews were tape recorded. They were undertaken using fixed questions allowing unstructured answers.

As far as possible I wanted the persons interviewed to talk freely, so as not to limit their answers to include only what I already knew or could imagine about the girls. This turned out to be a fruitful method. I came to see the girls from new angles and learned that there was much that I had been unaware of. However, this method suggests that the data obtained were not suitable to present statistically to any great extent. Similarly, the data are not automatically "complete." For instance, when some parents answer a certain question without mentioning a very usual problem, this may be because this particular girl does not have this problem — but, on the other hand, it may be because this problem is seen as a behavior which has become so natural with this girl that the parents no longer see it as a deviation or something worth mentioning. This uncertainty is built into the method.

When it came to recollections of early infancy and of what happened during the early stages of the disorder, the parents' answers vary in nature and quality. This is often because, for some of them, this period occurred very recently, but for others, whose children are older, it was in the more distant past. For example, some parents can point out exactly in what respects the children were delayed in their psychomotor development, whereas others cannot remember so precisely, but still claim that the girls were "later than" or "different from" their siblings, or "more slow" or "less demanding." I have judged this latter form of information to be as valuable as the more detailed reminiscences.

Although the persons interviewed were asked to talk freely, it is quite remarkable how well their answers coincided — which may indicate that the correlation could have been still better had there been fixed alternatives for the answers. Within certain areas it may also be of interest to follow up this study with more detailed questions and precise alternatives for the answers to get wider and more certain knowledge.

In addition, I personally have worked with a couple of girls with Rett syndrome. One was a student in my class for 1 year, when she was 15. The student previously mentioned is now 13 and was in my class for 6 years. The conclusions presented in this report are a synthesis of the information received from interviews, observations, and my own practical work.

I have chosen to report mainly on matters common enough or concerning so many of the girls in the study that one can say they are "part of the picture" of Rett syndrome. I will first give a general outline of the development and progress of the disorder. Then I will present my data in the following way: a brief presentation of the girls in the study; a more detailed account of typical symptoms and behaviors; and guidelines for treatment and teaching.

A GENERAL OUTLINE OF THE DEVELOPMENT AND PROGRESS IN RETT SYNDROME

2

Professor Bengt Hagberg and Dr. Ingegerd Witt-Engerström have written a general outline of Rett syndrome in which the disorder is described as consisting of four stages.

Stage 1 can begin somewhere between 6 and 18 months of age, and the duration is generally a few months. Psychomotor development slows down and stagnates. Until then the child has progressed and acquired new skills but perhaps somewhat later than normal and at a slower rate. Gradually, an increasing lack of attention is noticeable and the child becomes more inactive. Nonspecific, episodic hand-waving may occur together with functional use of hands. The rate of skull growth decelerates.

Stage 2 falls somewhere between 1 and 3 years of age and lasts for some weeks or months. It is characterized by a general developmental deterioration with regression and loss of acquired skills. The regression may be sudden and dramatic or more protracted in its course. The girl appears isolated and sometimes psychotic/autistic. She gives the impression of severe dementia. She stops babbling and using the few words she has learned. She loses her acquired hand skills and the ability to use the hands functionally, instead the typical hand stereotypies manifest themselves. The gross motor skills are better preserved although often affected; the girl becomes unsteady with uncoordinated and jerky movements.

Stage 3 can last for many years, from preschool into the school years. The girl no longer regresses in her development but stabilizes at the level reached. The autistic features diminish and the girl shows a better emotional contact with her surroundings. Gross motor abilities are still largely preserved and are only very slowly and successively deteriorating. The jerky truncal ataxia with poor muscle coordination is prominent. Epileptic seizures are common.

Stage 4 is characterized by improved emotional contact. The epileptic seizures are not so problematic and are easier to control with medication. The gross motor deterioration accelerates and weakness, wasting, spasticity and scoliosis force most of the girls into a nonambulatory life, making them bound to a wheelchair, although there are exceptions. Trophic foot disturbances are common, leading to cold, bluish and swollen feet.

Thus, the disorder leads to certain specific symptoms and handicaps. The course of the disease is predetermined but there are variations in the visible onset of the disorder as well as in the speed and degree of the deterioration. Consequently, two girls of the same age can present two totally different pictures of the disorder.

A BRIEF PRESENTATION OF THE INDIVIDUALS IN THE STUDY

3

The 39 individuals are in most cases severely disabled. Their gross motor handicaps worsen with increasing age. Nevertheless, 14 of them are able to walk unaided, although not without problems. In addition, 4 younger girls walk with varying degrees of support and 1 young girl moves around by crawling. Twenty of the girls are wheelchair-bound, but 6 of these are able to walk a short distance with aid. Many of those girls now sitting in a wheelchair were previously able to walk independently, although 9 of them never learned to walk at all (this does not include the youngest group, 2-6 years).

Thirty-two are suffering from scoliosis, which is more prominent with increasing age. Of these girls, 15 are so handicapped that they cannot sit without support.

Table 1 Mobility and Scoliosis						
Age (years)	Group (n)	Scoliosis (n)	In wheelchair (n)	Walk unaided (n)	Walk with support (n)	Sit without support (n)
2-6	7	2	-	2	4	7
7-11	13	13	7	6	-	8
12-16	8	8	5	3	-	7
17-21	7	7	5	2	-	3
22-26	2	2	2	-	-	-
27-29	2	2	1	1	-	1
Total	39	34	20	14	4	26

Almost all the girls and women have had physiotherapy. How much physiotherapy the girls are offered is, of course, a question of individual needs, but also a question of where they live — in some districts the resources are very limited. After an introductory period, the physiotherapists generally serve as consultants, while the practical treatment is carried out by other personnel or parents.

Of the girls, 28 have weekly swim sessions in warm pools; the parents of girls not having access to pool baths often request it. Only 10 girls go horseback riding regularly, but in this case, too, many parents and teachers ask for this opportunity to be made more available.

All the girls of the study have severe fine motor handicaps. Only in 3 of them is a fairly functional grasp preserved, and 2 of these also succeeded in maintaining their grip for a while; they have a rudimentary pincer grasp. Nineteen girls have a quick rake grasp which they seldom utilize and which often proves unsuccessful. Only 7 of these 19 are capable of keeping an object in the hand, and when they can, it is only for a very short while. Of the cases where it is possible to decide, 14 are right-handed and 15 are left-handed, but 4 of the latter are beginning to change preference and are tending to become right-handed.

Twenty five girls had a skilled and functional pincer grasp before falling ill. Five of them had a palmar grasp and 7 an opposed thumb-grasp, while in a few cases the parents are unsure.

Table 2
Hand Motor Skills

Age Group	total	Grasp		Stereotypies			
		Pincer grasp	Rake grasp	Hands together	Hands apart	Intense	Quiet
(years)	(n)	(n)	(n)	(n)	(n)	(n)	(n)
2-6	7	-	4	6	1	7	-
7-11	13	-	9	8	5	7	6
12-16	8	-	4	5	3	5	3
17-21	7	(2)	2	6	1	2	5
22-26	2	-	-	2	-	-	2
27-29	2	-	-	2	-	1	1
Total	39	(2)	19	29	10	22	17

All the girls have stereotypic hand movements. In most cases the stereotypies slow down with increasing age. Twenty nine hold their hands together in washing, picking, or clasping movements; 10 keep their hands apart and stereotypically touch some other part of the body (face, chest, shoulder). Both hands are, however, engaged in the stereotypies even when working apart. Hand-to-mouth behavior is common in both groups.

All the girls who need them, have aids for compensating for their gross motor disabilities. When it comes to fine motor aids, however, an altogether different picture emerges. Only in some 10 cases has an attempt been made to compensate for the impaired hand function by using adapted easy-to-grip items or various types of switches.

Five of the girls have various types of restraints in order to prevent the stereotypies (splints, braces). Seven have previously used such restraints.

It should be noted that when the girls are not compensated for their fine motor handicaps, it is not due to a lack of will or commitment on the part of their caregivers, but rather a lack of detailed understanding of the real nature of the individual handicaps. Only a few of them have been in contact with occupational therapists, the persons best suited to find practical solutions to hand-motor problems.

The girls and women cannot act independently in daily activities and routines. Even those who can take part more actively in the eating situation need a great deal of attention and help from their caregivers. Most of them are very interested in and fond of food and show great eagerness (and impatience) at the dining table. They participate by looking, opening their mouth, and reaching for a spoon or the arm of an adult. Three girls are capable of holding a spoon by themselves and lifting it to their mouths; 1 of these also manages to scoop the food on to the spoon. These 3 girls are also capable of holding and drinking from a glass. All the others are fed, although training in participation is carried through in some cases. Of these girls 5 or 6 sometimes try to eat bread or pieces of fruit with their fingers, and they do succeed in this to a fairly large extent; a few of them are also able to hold a glass by themselves.

All the girls use diapers. However, many of them seem to have made the connection and eliminate when placed on the toilet. In some cases the adults can tell when the girls are wet and need a dry diaper, but none of the girls is active in communicating this message.

The girls need total physical assistance when they dress and undress. They can take part by lifting a foot, stretching an arm out into the sleeve, and in some cases they are able to take off a cap. More commonly, however, they do not participate at all. In fact, many people point out that the girls, rather than cooperating actively, resist in these situations, making the whole affair still more complicated.

The girls are also affected by other handicaps and problems. Twenty-five of them suffer from epileptic seizures, varying in type and degree of severity. Gastrointestinal disturbances are common; 32 of those studied have problems with constipation, and 14 suffer from regular vomiting. Many lose weight periodically without any apparent reason, such as altered or diminished intake of food. The wasting is more common and permanent among the oldest girls and women.

Table 3
Some Problems which Occur Frequently

Age (years) (n)	Group total (n)	Seizures (n)	Constipation (n)	Vomiting (n)
2-6	7	-	5	5
7-11	13	10	9	4
12-16	8	8	8	2
17-21	7	5	7	3
22-26	2	1	2	-
27-29	2	1	1	-
Total	39	25	32	14

None of the girls in the study has impaired hearing or severe visual handicaps although 17 girls do have minor visual problems — 8 are far-sighted, 5 are near-sighted, 4 have errors of refraction, and 1 has a cataract. Of these girls, 11 wear glasses. Not all of those studied have had ophthalmological examinations. Twenty-one have or have had a squint. Reportedly, many older girls had a more prominent squint when younger and now have only a slight squint when they are tired or for some reason weakened.

Table 4 Visual Problems							
Age total (years)	Group (n)	Far- sighted (n)	Near- sighted (n)	Others (n)	Glasses (n)	Squint (n)	Earlier squint (n)
2-6	7	1	-	-	1	5	1
7-11	13	2	1	1	4	3	4
12-16	8	2	1	2	4	1	1
17-21	7	3	1	-	2	1	3
22-26	2	-	1	-	-	-	-
27-29	2	-	1	2	-	-	2
Total	39	8	5	5	11	10	11

In addition to the hand stereotypies, there are several other stereotypic behaviors. Of those in the study, 29 have spells and periods of hyperventilation, 9 are "air-swallowers" with an abdominal distension as a result (so-called bloating), and 14 have spells of breath holding. The stereotypies involving breathing irregularities are not as permanent as the hand stereotypies, and they occur more sporadically.

Twenty-one of the girls grind their teeth. This behavior, too, is a more sporadic one: 11 have previously engaged in teeth grinding but are not doing so at present.

The girls are considered to have a great sleep requirement. All of them sleep at least 9 hours a night. They do not need less sleep with increasing age, rather the opposite. Daily naps are common with almost all of them, regardless of age. About ten of them are reported to be able to fall asleep abruptly, in the middle of some activity, and then wake up in the same sudden way, becoming alert independently without any need in getting themselves roused. About half of the girls have or have had periods when they, on waking up, seem to be amazed, "as if they do not know where they are." They do not seem to be unhappy, but may look scared — or enchanted. Almost half of them also have periods of night terrors, or they may awaken from a nap crying inconsolably. On these occasions, some of the girls have fits of laughter instead of crying.

Twenty-one subjects have had screaming attacks or spells of sudden and inexplicable unconsolable crying during the early stages

Table 5 Other Stereotypies					
Age Group (years) (n)	Hyper- ventilation (n)	Breath- holding (n)	Bloating (n)	Teeth grinding (n)	Earlier teeth grinding (n)
2- 6 7	3	2	1	5	1
7-11 13	12	5	1	9	3
12-16 8	6	4	3	4	2
17-21 7	5	3	4	1	4
22-26 2	2	-	-	1	-
27-29 2	1	-	-	1	1
Total 39	29	14	9	21	11

of the disorder. There are also ten cases of these sudden and unconsolable crying spells among the older girls and women. Members of the family and other persons close to the patients often interpret these crying attacks as a manifestation of pain, generally stomach complaint, or as some kind of epileptic seizure.

Although all girls show unusual interactional behavior, they are all interested in making contact with their surroundings despite the fact that they are severely handicapped in communicating. They can convey feelings, needs, and wishes, but do not do so in the conventional manner. Even girls who do make a lot of sounds and who may have retained some words do not use them for the purpose of communication. The older the girl, the more silent she is in general and the fainter her signals. The girls are described by many people as "talking with their eyes." Twenty-five of them have marked eye-pointing, but even the others use their eyes for communicating. The eye-pointing does not — like other signals — fade with increasing age.

Ten respond with self-injurious behavior (e.g. biting their hands, banging their heads) when disappointed and frustrated and in situations where they cannot explain themselves or do what they want or have things their own way.

Seven of the girls in the study have previously responded with self-injury but have later given up this behavior. Only a few show, or have shown, self-injurious behavior not connected with any specific

Table 6 Verbal Capacity					
Age (years)	Total (n)	Have been using: 1-word phrases (n)	2-word phrases (n)	Never used words (n)	Still using words (n)
2- 6	7	5	1	1	2
7-11	13	8	1	4	4
12-16	8	7	-	1	1
17-21	7	4	1	2	-
22-26	2	2	-	-	-
27-29	2	-	-	2	-
Total	39	26	3	10	7

situation, for instance, through hand stereotypies so violent that they have hurt themselves in this way.

The girls are often described as "creatures of habit." Routines are very important to them and they manage best in familiar and well-known situations. When it is important to them they are capable of making very quick and consistent associations, though sometimes incorrect ones. Also, when it is important to them they can display a very vivid and "long-lasting" memory. The people around the girls are often uncertain of how much the girls really understand, but all agree that they are capable of greater understanding than their level of functioning suggests.

It is usual for the girls to show great fluctuations in their behavior, when it comes to mood as well as to performance. Thirty-five of them show pronounced fluctuations of this kind. These fluctuations are described as originating within the patients, and not primarily as being caused by external circumstances.

Housing and Schools

Of the 39 girls in the study, 31 live with their parents, 5 are in public institutions, and another 3 in anthroposophical curative institutions (similar to establishments organized by the "Camphill Movement").

All the girls not living in their parental homes still have close contact with their parents. The families with daughters living at home often have access to the local services of various kinds of convalescent care homes for some weekends or some nights a week. In some families a helping person is available during the day. The solution chosen is, of course, dependent on the situation of the individual family, but also on the part of the country that they live in, as practice and resources differ considerably from one district to another.

The children of preschool age all have access to an ordinary daycare center or preschool. The girls are integrated into the type of group considered best suited to their biological age and developmental level. How successfully the integration turned out was dependent on the individual girl as well as on the willingness of staff to adjust their educational guidelines to her. All the girls in daycare centers have personal assistants, and generally the girl and the assistant have the opportunity to leave the group for some quiet place whenever the girl needs to do so. Here the girl and the assistant can be in one-to-one contact, and usually this is where the assistant, the teacher, and the physiotherapist do most of their work.

The three girls living in anthroposophical institutions also have their education and training there. They have access to a special teaching situation with, for example, curative eurhythmics. On the other hand, they do not have the same opportunities for physiotherapy and physical training as the other girls have.

The rest of the school-age girls are enrolled in public schools for severely mentally retarded children. Since they usually are seriously multihandicapped, they are often placed in various types of special classes. Class placement depends on whether the predominant problem is physical or mental. The classes are small, with generally three or four students in each. Usually there are two or three staff members. A 1:1 staff/student ratio is not unusual and is often considered necessary when eating, swimming, riding, or any activity outside the classroom takes place. If the permanent number of staff is not sufficient, temporary help is sought to reach the required number of helpers in the class. Even the 5 older females working in day centers are placed in small groups with a large number of staff.

All of the preschoolers have personal assistants, but only two of the school-age girls have their own personal assistant. In practice, however, a system of assigning the same adult to the same student in class is often used.

Most of the girls have a full-time school week. There are some exceptions; for example, if the child is starting school and needs a period of acclimatization, or because she has a long and taxing journey to school. There are also a few girls who have a reduced school week because of their poor physical health and extreme tiredness. Only one girl has not been in school at all, but has been trained at home by a visiting teacher, something which has proved to be a very good solution.

AN ACCOUNT OF TYPICAL SYMPTOMS AND BEHAVIORS

4

Those with Rett syndrome are, above all, individuals, and should always be treated as such.

Like other people, they have their strengths as well as their weaknesses; whether they are children or grown-ups, handicapped or non-handicapped.

Each human is an individual who has characteristics that are unique as well as features which are common with other people's. Classifying a person's characteristics and behaviors is something that can only be done on paper. In real life each human is a whole entity and must be treated so, without other persons distinguishing and emphasizing only some features, or paying attention to parts rather than to the whole.

Nevertheless, in order to understand and treat those with Rett syndrome in the best possible way, it is necessary to know more exactly their true condition. For this purpose I have chosen to discuss in the next chapters some problems and handicaps which are so common among the girls in the study that they must be considered characteristic of the disorder.

I will discuss these prominent features of the girls and women under the following headings: (1) deficiencies in perception and sensory integration; (2) stereotypic behaviors; (3) apraxia; (4) severe motor disabilities; (5) difficulties in coordination; (6) mental retardation; (7) communication disorders; (8) "emotional channels"; (9) large fluctuations in behavior; (10) emotional reactions; (11) insecure identity.

1   Deficiencies in Perception and Sensory Integration

Individuals with Rett syndrome have difficulties taking in, interpreting, and integrating sensory impressions, from the outer world as well as from their own bodies. Not only do the girls have difficulty in sorting, integrating, and choosing among the multitude of impressions — they may also have problems in modulating the strength of the sensory impressions they receive. This means that a sound that is in itself not very strong may be perceived as extremely loud or, on the contrary, that something that "ought" to be perceived as strong — pain, for instance — may not be perceived at all.

We still do not know very much about how early these difficulties begin. According to the parents, many of the girls seemed to be in some way "generally inert" early in their infancy, showing a lack of interest in the outer world, including an apparent perceptual indifference. Others exhibited a very "limited selectivity" where only certain particular stimuli seemed to give rise to strong reactions, positive or negative. Most of the girls, however, showed a dramatic change when they entered stage two of the disorder. Previously having lived in a fairly sheltered and understandable world, they then found themselves in some kind of sensory and perceptual chaos. The signals from their own bodies and from the outer world seemed to overwhelm and confuse them, instead of giving them useful information.

One mother tells it as follows: "Soon after her first birthday she changed totally in just a couple of weeks. She became inactive and quiet, stopped playing and babbling and lost the few words she had learned. She became afraid of everything — sounds, strangers, water. When she got frightened she screamed hysterically and could not be consoled. If you tried to lift her up she became desperate, fighting to get away. She could no longer sit on a chair, but had to eat on the floor. She only felt safe and secure in her bed and with her doll."

Other parents give similar information: "She stopped grasping objects from one day to another. When you put a spoon in her hand she reacted as if it was stinging her." — "She started vomiting when eating — it seemed as if she could not feel the food in her mouth and got

startled when it fell down her throat." — "She was scared of everything — sounds, changes of position, new environments. If you just
looked at her she started to scream. We could not carry her or touch
her hands. She cried inconsolably at night and scratched her body until
it was raw. She had difficulty in eating, and although she became very
choosy about food, she often threw it up." — "She screamed and
screamed and seemed to be very frightened. We did not know if she
was in pain or was hallucinating or having some kind of epileptic
seizure."

Explains erroneous psychosis diagnosis!

The parents describe how their daughters' existence turned into
a frightening chaos, impossible to handle. Each girl somehow seemed
to be hypersensitive to everything — the food felt strange in her
mouth; the water felt disgusting touching her body; the sounds
became dangerous in her ears; someone moving or touching her was
suddenly threatening.

This oversensitivity could be replaced by moments or even days
when the child seemed to be quite unresponsive, and unaware of many
normal signals. This might be explained by a genuine change in
sensory capability. It might also be explained as a defense — when the
girl's life seemed to be too threatening, she cut off all the lines of
sensory communication with the outside world. Many parents also
describe this behavior as the child's "being completely turned either
outwards to the outer world or inwards to the signals from her own
body."

Gradually the girls seem to come out of this chaos. Their
sensitivity appears to be more normal and their ability to interpret
different signals improve. Through their experiences, they have been
able to sort things out, find structure and understanding in their lives,
and learn a variety of ways to handle their many difficulties. However,
the children's ability to perceive and to integrate sensory stimuli will
never be normal. Their susceptibility to sensory impressions will not
become uniform, but fluctuated with internal and external conditions,
causing the girls' behavior to seem very inconsistent: "Sometimes she
hears the slightest sound," says a parent, "and other times she would
not respond to a bomb being dropped beside her."

Even later in life, the sensory susceptibility may be so marked
that the girls run the risk of being overwhelmed by a multitude of

stimuli and again land up in chaos. In unfamiliar situations, the girl's interest is great but so too is the quantity of unsorted signals, and thus the demands on her are particularly high. She has to take in a lot of impressions, relate them to each other and, by processing and interpreting, find a structure in this new situation, to which it is possible for her to understand and respond. In such a situation it may be impossible to take in all the information simultaneously. In the same way as the girl has to give priority to what she will take in, she may also have to choose how she will take it in. Exploring a situation actively with both sight and hearing; for instance, may not be possible — and then the girl has to choose one of them, even if she is not doing this by any conscious operation.

Sometimes this process can manifest itself in extreme ways. When one of my students was new at school, she used her sight in such an active way that it totally repressed the other senses. We knew she was not deaf, but we had difficulty hanging on to this knowledge when we saw how she acted. She neither twitched nor blinked when we tried to provoke her with various kinds of sounds or noises. At home, where she was familiar with the setting and the people, she did hear just perfectly. (As she did in school when she got used to it!). During this period there were many situations totally puzzling to us. As long as we remembered to communicate with the girl through her "sight channel" however, everything turned out fine. The alternative for this student might have been total openness to the outer world which may have resulted in emotional chaos — or total rejection of the outer world which may have led to emotional isolation and lack of contact.

Sight

There are also some peculiarities in how individuals with Rett syndrome use their senses. In my study, none of the individuals had severe sight or hearing impairments, but minor visual problems had been confirmed in nearly half of them. (Not all in the study, however, had received an ophthalmological examination.) Most of the visual problems were minor degrees of near-sightedness (myopia) or farsightedness (hyperopia). Not all those students with visual problems wore glasses. Indeed, as previously mentioned, more than half of them have had a squint for some period of time.

Regardless of squinting or other visual problems, many girls use their sight in an unusual manner. For instance, they use a peripheral gaze — they do not look straight at an object but catch it from the corner of their eye or in the fringe of their visual field. "She ogles" — "She glances furtively" — "She sees without looking" — "She never looks out but still knows where she is going" are different ways of describing this peculiarity. When the girls visually approach something new and unfamiliar, they often do so gradually and step by step, swiftly casting an eye on it, breaking the glance, rapidly looking again, looking away. This behavior is repeated until they have sufficiently surveyed the situation and can begin a more careful exploration of it. Then, in contrast, they may gaze very steadily and often want to look very close, whether or not they were being assessed as nearsighted.

The girls without visual problems are described as having "good sight," both at near and far distances. However, many parents point out that the girls look "either-or;" that is, they may abruptly shift from looking very close to looking into the distance, or vice versa, "not seeing" things in-between. Likewise the girls can have difficulty in visually following an object moving away from or towards themselves. As soon as a conscious effort is required to follow an object, moving either laterally or vertically, they also have problems. In these situations the girls do not move their eyes smoothly, but adjust their gaze in a series of jerky step-wise movements. In "natural" situations — for instance, when the girls are looking at people moving about the room or at tasty food being moved on the table — they appear to display no such difficulties.

When the girls examine an unfamiliar environment there are certain things that catch their attention more than others. Later on these things may be important details in identifying the place in question. Things selected in this way are objects that provide a distinct figure-ground effect by sharp contrasts or clear outlines (e.g. dark doors against a white wall, the control knobs on the stove, big clocks with clear hands, distinct letters on backs of books, a patterned pillow on the sofa). The girls are attracted to light (lamps, the sun), motion, moving light (like mirrors, glitter and tinsels, candles). They also select eyes and eye-like objects (people, pictures of people, the doll with the biggest or most distinct eyes). All these things tend, through their perceptual impact, to break the girls' concentration by constantly catching their eyes. Depending on the situation, these things "disturb the girl" — "fascinate the girl," or "serve as her security." Attending to movements, eye-like objects, and sharp contrasts is characteristic but not unique to these girls. This selective attention was once crucial to our survival and is programmed in the deepest layers of the brain. Now these preferences are best observed in infant children and in brain-damaged persons. In the rest of us, they are overlaid by experience — we are not so much at the mercy of our sensory impressions and we tend to give things a significance from their meaning. As time passes, the girl's experiences, of course, will also help her to make such interpretations. The living room may be "the room with the tape recorder." If there is no such thing to rely upon, the living room may continue to be "the room with the patterned carpet" and in that case the carpet will be very important to the girl.

A recurring feature is that the ambulatory girls show great hesitation facing obstacles. They seem to have difficulty in estimating the height of a step and may need a lot of concentration to negotiate a threshold. Some of them do not dare to step up at all. Even when there are no real differences in level, they often show great uncertainty, for instance, when there are lines painted on the floor or a joint between two different types of flooring or a changeover from a gravel path to a lawn. One mother describes how she can let her daughter enjoy her freedom in the garden without constantly watching over her, with the help of a rope that has been stretched round the garden just a little above the ground. The rope is fixed so low that the girl should be able to climb over it easily, but she seems to perceive it as insurmountable. Another example is a little girl trying in vain to get up from the floor. This girl can walk but she cannot rise to a standing position without the help of some high object, a chair or similar object. Neither does she crawl willingly. With great efforts she crawls towards the doorstep, which she probably perceives as "high." She then persistently tries to pull herself up to standing, using the doorstep as an aid, which, of course, results in failure.

Hearing

The problem with sound impressions is that they are mostly transient, and consequently more difficult to interpret correctly if not repeated. They are also more difficult than visual impressions to sort out and to "approach" step by step. Many of these girls become unhappy (or overreact in some other way) in a setting that is too noisy, or when listening to blaring or complex music without an easily-found rhythm or melody. At the same time, sound impressions are very important to them. Together with sight, hearing seems to be the sense mostly concerned with sorting out and organizing the external world. These girls are very clever at interpreting familiar sounds, meaningful to them, and in such cases their range is large. One little girl, for example, always goes to the bathroom when she hears the bath tub faucet turned on, regardless of where she is in the house. Another girl always knows when the TV is turned on, even if the parents try to do it secretly. She hears the little click and turns her head in the right direction.

On the other hand, a child with Rett syndrome can find it very difficult, for instance, to play hide-and-seek and to understand where her mother's voice is coming from, even if she just stands behind the door. With each new hiding place the situation is novel and the child has no previous experiences to help her.

The girls' endeavors to understand and bring order sometimes give rise to failures in association — an unknown sound is con-nected with the wrong cause. In a daycare center, for instance, we once sat talking over a cup of coffee. The girl who was the subject of my visit was sitting safely on her mother's lap. Then it was time to pay and put money in the collection box. The money made a nice jingle and the girl immediately responded by ceasing her stereotypic hand movements. The jingle went on for a while but the girl did not turn her head in that direction, but instead looked at me and then laughed. Her interest continued even when the sound had disappeared and when we rose from the table, she went up to me and laughed—maybe she wanted me to repeat that funny jingling. Earlier during the coffee-break she had not paid me any particular attention or in any way singled me out. In this case, the girl made an incorrect association, but she made it — from her point of view — in a logical way. Unknown sound — unknown person.

High and shrill sounds are often very frightening to these children. Other sounds, too, coming suddenly and unexpectedly and which are not in the girls' "answer book" may be very startling or even provoke the opposite reactions (for instance, the girls start to roar with laughter). One child suddenly became afraid of the cars driving on the road outside the garden. She had not previously reacted in this way and she was very fond of cars. Now it seemed as if she did not hear the sound of the cars at all at the beginning and then suddenly perceived it far too strongly, and she could neither interpret nor locate it — she did not understand what it was or where it came from. She became terribly frightened and tried to run in all directions at once. Her mother turned her towards the road and explained to her that it was only a car passing by. When the girl got the word "car" and saw the car by herself she could make an association and give the sound a meaning again. Her mother learned to tell her in advance "now there is a car coming" and the girl gradually overcame her fear.

Pain

The girls are generally described as having a high pain threshold, even if their sensitivity in this area, too, seems to vary from time to time. They also have difficulty in expressing the pain they actually do feel. In many cases the reaction to pain is delayed. Sometimes a child does not show any reactions other than tensing herself immensely or becoming very tired after a while. When analyzing the descriptions of the pain reactions more thoroughly, one can see that pain "from within" (stomach complaint, headache) seems to be more strongly perceived than pain "from without" (injections, pinches, bites). More prolonged pain from without (several injections, e.g.) also seems to be experienced more powerfully than a pain of shorter duration, when one sometimes gets the impression that the girls do not "catch up." In addition, different parts of the body seem to be of different sensitivity. If the girl has her hands pinched she may not react at all as strongly as if she has her cheeks pinched. Several parents report that when their daughter has fallen backwards and bumped her head she has not shown any reaction whatsoever; whereas when she has fallen forwards, she has cried in despair.

Tactile Impressions

On the whole, the girls in the study are very sensitive and careful about their faces. Often they do not like to have their faces touched and many parents have worked out little rhymes and games to make this possible. When one touches their faces they often respond with big grimaces involving eyes, nose, and mouth. When asked if there was anything these girls truly disliked, many people answered that they hate wind, snow, rain, and water splashing in their faces. Almost all of the girls often rub their eyes and face and scratch their hair and ears — sometimes when they are tired, sometimes without any apparent reason.

About one-third of the girls were spontaneously described as having a "sensitive mouth." For example, they are extremely reluctant to have their teeth brushed. Still more of them demonstrate great sensitivity at mealtimes, but they are more sensitive on some days than on others, a fact that makes them seem unpredictably choosy. Some days a girl will readily eat food which, on other occasions, will make her feel queasy or vomit, or which she will spit out. Many times it is easier for her to accept food after the first few spoonfuls when the mouth has been "accustomed" to the food and when she has had time to analyze the tactile impressions and perhaps associate them with a positive taste sensation. The temperature of the food is important too; it must neither be too hot nor too cold.

With the kind of oversensitivity these girls display, the texture of the food seems to play a more important role than the sensations of taste and smell. "Prickly" food (like lettuce, parsley, rye crisp), heterogeneous food (occasional big pieces in strained food), and things like peas, rice, macaroni are examples of food the girls often overreact to, responding with strong aversion, even if they like food and are able to chew well. For the most part, this sensitivity is not a major problem since most of them, due to their poor oral motor skills, are served mashed and homogeneous food. Generally it is more difficult for them to swallow liquids than solid food. Many interpret this as meaning the girls "do not feel that they have something in the mouth" but the real cause may well be their general apraxia and disturbances of muscular coordination.

Ulrika is almost always happy at swimming sessions. Her difficulties with balance, however, remain even in the water.

When Katarina tilts her first to one side and then to the other, Ulrika is not quite "with it."

Her facial expression and her whole body shows that she finds this tilting disgusting.

Afterwards, she looks quite exhausted. This movement has to be repeated several times before Ulrika finds the rhythm and is able to enjoy it.

Balance

Individuals with Rett syndrome often show poor balance and have difficulties in controlling position and movements. It may be difficult and frightening to walk on uneven surfaces. If she happens to step on a threshold or on something lying on the floor, a girl may "get stuck", not being able to move at all. She may need help to "get loose," if only with words and reassuring hands. One of the girls in the study did not dare to move at all if she felt water under her feet, however little. These subjects are afraid of sudden changes of body position and some of them have a very pronounced fear of heights. Many of the girls react with discomfort and fear to varying body positions (lying down on their back or face, standing on all fours) and they struggle to get back to a "normal" position by diligently lifting their head and shoulders from the surface when in a prone or supine position. They do not like it when other people handle their bodies, and dressing and physical therapy are examples of situations which can be very trying to the girls and to their surroundings as well. Those who can walk may appear extremely afraid of falling. They may begin to shake as soon as they see another child approaching or they may not want to walk at all unless they have large empty spaces around them or a wall to cling to.

2   Stereotypic Behaviors

Hand mannerisms are characteristic of Rett syndrome and these stereotypies are common to all the girls and women, regardless of age and course of disorder. Often the stereotypies start with nonspecific waves or odd postures of the hands. Then she may begin to lick one of her hands and eventually she engages both hands in a particular pattern of motion. The movements are intense and the hands often interact with movements of the mouth and tongue; for instance, she will use her fingers to pull or twist her tongue which at the same time is moved in and out of her mouth. In most cases the girls hold their hands together in the midline of the body, in clapping, wringing, "washing" movements. Some girls, however, have their hands apart, working independently. In both cases, the movements are not symmetrical and each hand has its own individual task. Nevertheless, the hands interact in a certain pattern, repeated over and over again and in a specific rhythm. The movement pattern of the individual girl is not very extensive but the rhythm can be intensified or subdued. The stereotypies diminish in size and intensity over the years and are no longer centered on the mouth to the same extent as in early life. Instead of the hands unceasingly seeking each other out in large and active movements, they settle down together. The older girls often sit with their hands together in a firm grip that is hard to loosen; the fingers tapping and picking at each other with small and fine movements. The stereotypic hand movements continue to be more active and intense, however, with the girls who are mobile and have a more rapid "psychic tempo."

The stereotypies differ from those seen in children with infantile autism. These children often involve objects in their stereotypies and they utilize these objects in a very skillful — though not functional — manner, twirling and fluttering them. Girls with Rett syndrome do not involve any objects in their stereotypies, their hands are solely engaged with one another or with other parts of the body [Ingegerd Witt-Engerström, 1987]. Neither do they use their hands for visual stimulation, which is common among autistic children. One does not get the impression that these girls' stereotypies are used primarily for self-stimulation or as a shield against other people. On the contrary, the girls themselves have difficulty in breaking their stereotypies, even in situations where they apparently want to do so.

In most cases the stereotypic hand movements are continuous even if they sometimes are more subdued. They are not replaced by, but on the contrary affect and restrain a more normal use of the hands. When the girls are inactivated or in some kind of stressful situation, the stereotypies increase in intensity. Positive stress (like eagerness or curiosity) has the same effect as has negative stress (demands, discomfort, pain). The stereotypies are subdued or totally cease when the girls are distracted by something else; for instance, when they are

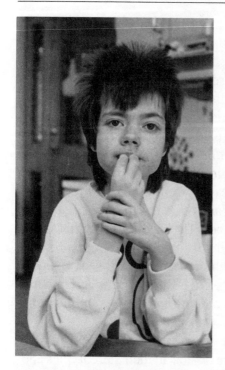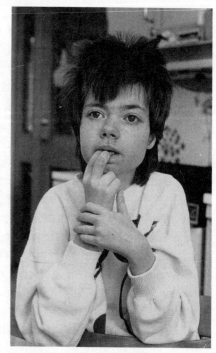

Ulrika's stereotypies involve her mouth. The fingers of her right hand are placed more or less deeply into her mouth. One can see that especially the forefinger and the middle finger are involved. These fingers are also thicker as a result of swellings and callouses.

actively engaged in taking in information from the external world through sight and hearing. The stereotypies are not present during sleep.

Mouth grimaces are very common, especially in the younger girls. They make stretching and twisting movements of the lower jaw, lips, and tongue. They often "chew" saliva or bubble saliva between their lips. The grimaces sometimes interact with the hand mannerisms and are sometimes independent of them. Many parents state that the mouth grimaces are intensified if they try to stop the girls from engaging in their hand movements. Over the years the grimaces decrease, but by then they have often affected the girls' faces so that many of them resemble each other in their throat and mouth regions.

The left hand scratches and grips the right hand rhythmically, the grip alternately getting looser and tighter.

Other stereotypies are teeth-grinding and breathing irregularities such as hyperventilation, breath-holding, and bloating (when the girls swallow air with abdominal distension resulting). Sometimes the girls also have strange eye movements, such as closing their eyes, screwing up their eyes, raising and knitting their brows, or turning up the whites of their eyes.

These stereotypic behaviors do not occur with all the girls, and if they do, are not as permanent as the hand movements. Often they have occurred at some period but have then decreased or disappeared. Sometimes the behavior may return for a while. Hyperventilating and bloating often occur in stressful situations, but they may also be more intense at times without any obvious explanation.

3   Apraxia - "Want of Success"

Apraxia means an inability or difficulty in carrying out purposeful movements and actions in spite of normal mobility.

When Rett syndrome becomes manifest, the girls do not lose the ability to move their bodies, but they lose the ability to understand how to use their mobility. They have difficulty in responding to the external world in a proper manner, in much the same way as they have difficulty in taking in information from it. They no longer know how to transform a desire to act into the action itself.

The little girl who had a pincer grasp and had easily picked up the slightest thread from the floor, suddenly could not do this any more. One mother says: "She just stopped using her hands. If you put something in front of her she could, at best, grab it and throw it away." It is not certain that the girl was uninterested and really wanted to throw away her toy. Perhaps she wanted to grasp it and take it to her mouth and taste it. There was nothing wrong with her muscles or her mobility and her hand actually should have been able to manage it. But it did not — and perhaps it did something she had not even thought about. The child wants to act but cannot do so correctly. Not only has she problems in finding the proper movement, but also in finding the right strength and speed of movement. She has the same difficulty in adjusting her movements as she has in modulating her sensory impressions. Very often her desire to act does not result in any directed movement at all. Even if the girl wants to do something she cannot, because she does *not know how to do it*. She has been stricken with apraxia. This apraxia seems to have an overall effect, but its consequences are most evident in speech, fine motor skills, and complex gross motor skills. It is evident mainly in unfamiliar or trying situations.

One mother describes how her little girl stands in front of her toy shelf. Before she fell ill she liked very much to play there, manipulating and looking at the toys. Now again, she often stands there, looking and staring, hyperventilating, grinding her teeth, intensely rubbing her hands with her thumbs, her whole body stiff and tense. At last — sometimes — she succeeds in loosening one hand from its stereotypic movement pattern and then she hits some toy on the shelf so that it falls to the floor. Perhaps she intended to grasp it but the movement turned into hitting. Perhaps she intended to handle the toy, but her inability makes her just graze it and when she touches it, the movement is too hard and too quick — she knocks it down instead of grasping it.

Another little girl is standing by a tricycle. The other children at the daycare center are cycling, but this girl needs help. She circles round the tricycle, carefully watching it, she works with her tongue and wrings her hands hard together, she breathes heavily and stamps her feet. Now and then she moves a few steps away, placing herself with her back towards the tricycle, self-absorbed, engaging in intense hand stereotypies. Then she turns, looks at the tricycle again, looks away, looks back. She walks closer and begins to circle round it again. She looks more and more troubled and distressed. She rivets her eyes on the tricycle and watches it intensely as if she wanted the tricycle to place itself under her, since she cannot climb it. In this example the apraxia is total. The girl pulls herself together, concentrates and exerts herself to the utmost in order to solve the problem — but it all comes to nothing. She cannot make any directed movement towards the tricycle.

These are only two examples; there are many more. When these girls act, there are things happening before our eyes without our being able to see them — that is *our* handicap. We live in our frame of reference, we are prepared to see certain behaviors and to interpret certain signals — the rest passes unnoticed. Much of what we see as aimless behavior or unintentional movement may actually be very purposeful action — even if it does not lead to the desired end. Even if the girls in most cases fail in doing what they want to, many parents report how really happy the girls are when they do succeed.

Apraxia is one of the most fundamental handicaps in Rett syndrome. It affects almost all active behaviors of those afflicted. This in turn makes it very difficult to get a true picture of their intellectual capacity. The handicap — wanting but not being able to — also affects the emotional development, the identity, and the self-image of these girls.

4 Severe Motor Disabilities

The girls have limited mobility in all respects. Apart from the genuine motoric handicaps, their mobility is further impaired by apraxia, perceptual deficiencies, and difficulties in coordination. Both gross and fine motor skills are affected. The girls' oral motor skills are also strikingly poor. They have difficulty in biting hard enough on the "right" occasions. In order to bite off a piece of rye crisp, for instance, they may have to bite again and again before the bread is broken. The girls also have difficulty in chewing and swallowing. Most of those in the study need minced food and many of them eat mashed or strained food only. Of the 39 individuals in the study, 30 drool. Some of them produce such a large amount of saliva that they have problems with reddened and irritated skin, especially in cold weather.

⚹ Three Types of Motion

When analyzing the girls' movements one can see that there are mainly three types of motion. All of them are movements originating in the girls themselves — stereotypies, automatic movements, and "emotional motion."

Stereotypies. These are highly automated movements, performed so unconsciously that, regardless of situation, they can run parallel to most other activities.

Situation-Bound Automatic Movements. The kind of automation so natural to us, like walking, grasping, talking, is a problem for those with Rett syndrome. They often need to be "backed up" by certain situations telling them what to do and how to do it. Within these situations the movement pattern has been so exactly learned that it acts like a "reflex." The girls are so used to performing these movements that they make them without hesitation at the right time in the right situation. Always holding her hand on an adult's arm at meal-time or lifting her foot when pants are being taken off are examples of this kind of movement.

Unfortunately these movements have their limitations. They are not flexible and cannot be generalized to the extent often needed. While they serve well in one situation, they are inadequate or do not fit at all in others. Even if the behavior might be equally justified in another situation, it is not automatically transferred to that situation. The little girl who could touch the adult's arm in an eating situation may not be able to attract attention in this way on another occasion. Perhaps she cries or hits herself instead. The girl who lifts her foot when her pants are taken off may not be able to do the same movement when the pants are to be put on. Or she may perform the movement as soon as her pants are pulled down even if they are not to be taken off; for instance when changing diapers. Sometimes the girl continues to make a movement even when it no longer serves a useful purpose. The situation has "expired" but not the movement. There is always the risk of these kinds of automatic movements turning into stereotypies — to be used not only in the wrong context, but also out of any context at all.

Movements Arising from Emotional Involvement. Still, it is the girls' own inner driving force that most often provokes directed (and successful) movements. It is their own motivation that determines whether they are going to act at all and in that case which movement to perform. This motivation can be a positive wish but it can also be need, discomfort, necessity, or an inner compulsion. This is nothing consciously controlled by themselves, but originates spontaneously from their feelings in a particular situation or for an object. Consequently, one cannot successfully get the girl to grasp, for instance, by simply asking her to do so. In order to induce her to act one has to call forth her own motivation, appeal to her "emotional channels." Her hands are instruments of her heart, not of her head.

  The movement is best performed when the girls' inner driving force is so strong that their minds do not "catch up." Then all the blocked lines seem suddenly free for use. In such situations a girl who is "not able" to grasp, may quite simply grab her glass with both hands, raise it to her mouth and drink, and then neatly put it back on the table. She performs all this with smooth and coordinated movements. The people surrounding her are stunned — and so is she, if she becomes aware of what she did. If one asks her to repeat her performance she could not do so.

She does not "know" what she did. She only did what she had to do. In order to do the same thing again her desire/need has to be just as strong again and still remain "unconscious," and all the conditions have to be equally favorable. Hence, events like this do not happen very often; perhaps only once in a lifetime.

Gross Motor Skills

Many of the girls in the study have had an unusual crawling pattern. Only a few crawled normally with respect to time and movement pattern. Among the others, some had a normal pattern of movement but began crawling later than usual and also used this skill rather seldom. Most of the girls, however, began moving around later than normal and also chose other ways to move than the normal crawling pattern. They rolled, shuffled, made bunny-hops, or crawled in some strange uncoordinated manner. Still, many of them have made very good use of their skills — they moved quickly and over large areas. When the girls learned to walk, almost every one of them preferred walking and is no longer "able" to move in any other way. Walking seems to be a less complicated activity to these girls. Whether they are going to learn to walk at all depends, however, on their general muscle tone. Almost all the girls in the study who learned to walk also began walking very late, often after 15 months of age, with only a few exceptions.

When the disorder progresses, scoliosis gradually manifests itself, and an earlier low muscle tone can change into rigidity and spasticity. Trophic foot disturbances and cold and swollen feet with poor tactile perception are common additional handicaps. Due to all this, even those who have learned to walk and who have been walking independently for many years may have greater and greater difficulty in moving about and many of them will in the course of time be wheelchair bound.

Of the 39 girls in the study, 14 can walk by themselves. In addition, four of the small girls can walk with support and one little girl moves around by crawling. Twenty of the girls are wheelchair-bound, but six of them are still able to walk a short distance with support.

Many of the girls now sitting in a wheelchair have previously been able to walk independently. Only nine of those in the study never learned to walk (the group 2-6 years is not included in this number).

Lack of coordination and motor control, difficulty in shifting from one pattern of movements to another, and various perceptual and sensorimotor difficulties are traits present in all age groups, which prevent even those who can walk independently from fully utilizing this ability. They very seldom run and have difficulty in climbing up and down stairs. They do not move in a supple and smooth manner, and they often show difficulties with balance. They may need a great deal of practice in "simple and easy" tasks, like walking on uneven surfaces or rising from and sitting down on a chair. Truncal ataxia is rather common and the girls often walk with a stiff and broad-based gait. They often stagger when walking and even in a standing position they often rock and move their feet, or bend and tense their bodies in various ways. Many of them seem to utilize the position and rhythm of their hands to compensate for their poor balance. None of the girls can consciously use her motor ability to imitate the movements of others.

Of the 39 girls, 15 are not able to sit without support. In some cases this is due to poor muscle tone. With many of the girls, however, this difficulty is due to a scoliosis so severe that they cannot get their warped bodies balanced. Even those who are able to sit by themselves may have trouble in finding a state of equilibrium. When sitting on the floor, one of my students immediately lost her balance and fell when she moved her arms out from her body. When we offered her tempting items to grasp not only from a firm support (the floor) but also held in the air, and gradually moved the items higher and further away, by and by she learned to balance her body better and to stretch out her arms from her body without falling.

The girls' equilibrium reactions and protective response reactions are poor. None of them have backward protective reactions (but some of them have learned by experience to hold up their heads when falling backwards). In many cases the lateral and forward responses are undeveloped. Even those girls who display good protective reactions when examined cannot always make use of them in practice. When they fall, the responses are so delayed that they have no chance to avoid the shock.

Fine Motor Skills - Hand Function

The loss of acquired hand skills and a hand motor ability primarily used for stereotypic movements are the central symptoms in Rett syndrome.

Of the 39 girls in the study 25, had developed a fine pincer grasp before their hand function deteriorated. The parents report that many of the girls have been very clever in their motor skills and hand-eye coordination. "She was almost too clever, she picked up small little beads" — "She was like a vacuum cleaner, picking up every little scrap." Many of the girls have been able to turn over the pages of a book, or eat bread and butter, or finger-feed themselves.

When the children reach stage two of the disorder, they lose their earlier skills. They can no longer make their hands perform the movements they had made before. Descriptions vary as to how the girls ceased using their hands. In some cases the girls just slowly became more and more disinterested, stopped playing, and spent their time just sitting and looking, growing more and more passive. In other cases, the parents felt that their daughter's interest in using her hands was driven out by something else. "She learned to walk," one mother says, "and then there seemed to be no scope for anything else; she just walked and walked." Some parents describe how their daughter stopped grasping "from one day to another." — "She refused to hold her spoon any more, let it go and withdrew her hand as if the spoon had stung her."

Many of the girls act as if they perceive the signals from their hands as in some way being strange and different. They do not like other people to touch their hands or try to help them hand-over-hand to hold an object. The girls often lick and bite their hands and hold them in peculiar postures.

Children with Rett syndrome often totally stop using their hands for a while, and together with this inability of purposeful motor activity, hand-licking and waving turn into fully developed stereotypies. Later on the girls start trying to use their hands again, but they will never get their previous hand skills back. They are hindered by their apraxia as well as by their stereotypic hand movements. Some are also affected by ataxia with jerky uncoordinated arm and hand movements which impede them even further when they want to reach for a certain item. To an observer, the conscious, directed movements can be difficult to distinguish among the muddle of surrounding uncoordinated movements and stereotypies.

About a half of those in the study are still able to grasp but they seldom utilize this ability which is also a very poor one. The grasp is a sudden rake-grasp where the fingers do not have any active or specialized function. Often the grasp fails and turns into "striking" instead. If the subject does succeed in grasping, her grip loosens almost immediately. It is as difficult to hold an object as it is to grasp it. The same impairments that restrain the ability to grasp also restrain the ability to grip and maintain the grip.

Only a few of the girls in the study can grasp and hold an object for such a long time that they are able to perform a larger movement — like carrying something from one place to another or lifting the spoon to the mouth — but this ability is also poor and not constant. When it comes to feeding, the movements of the hand and the mouth are often synchronized, so that when the mouth opens the hand unclenches and the spoon will drop to the floor instead of going into the mouth. There is a remarkable difference when the girls grasp and hold on to something "live" — like another person's hand, hair, clothes, the fur of a dog — this is much easier.

A couple of the girls still have a primitive pincer grasp but they use it very seldom. None of them possesses the smooth and complex hand motor skills often seen in autistic children. The girls who most often use their hands for constructive aims do not have less intense or less frequent hand mannerisms. The opposite is rather the case, with the girls most often utilizing their hands in purposeful activities also having the most intense hand stereotypies.

With the course of the disorder the hand motor activities slow down and the stereotypic movements are correspondingly subdued. A growing spasticity makes it more difficult to grasp — but sometimes easier to keep an object in the hand. The rhythmic stereotypic movements which made the hand open and the object drop out of it no longer cause the same trouble. The stereotypies still continue, but they are slower and more limited.

Even if an increasing rigidity makes it more and more difficult for the girls to use their hands, they do not lose the desire to use them — provided that they can find a worthwhile reason for doing so. All the girls in the study are able to reach for an item and touch or knock it down. How they do this differs: some can extend their arms far out from the body; others have their arms more fixed. Some use one hand, some use both hands put together in a stereotypic posture, and there is a wide variation in how they touch an item — they may grasp, push, knock, or pat it.

When Ulrika wants to grasp something she looks at the selected object for a long time. Ulrika is very fond of glittering items - in this case it is spangled balls of papier maché. The paper muffin moulds prevent the balls from rolling away and make them easier to grip. They also give much tactile stimulation and the slightest move from Ulrika will make the moulds move and produce a nice sound.

Handedness

It is often difficult to decide whether the girls are right- or left-handed. Nevertheless, I was fairly sure about 29 of the 39 girls in the study: 14 of them are right-handed and 15 are left-handed. Among these 15 girls, however, four have begun to shift sides and are tending to become right-handed.

Only after a while does Ulrika put out her arm. She is used to grasping and her movements have become progressively slower over the years. She manages to put her hand forward and at the same time fix her eyes on the object. She gets hold of the desired item, but her grip is weak and her hand is clenching and unclenching rhythmically - the item will soon drop out of her hand. Note that only the hand used for grasping is released from the stereotypies. The other hand continues to move towards/into the mouth.

5 Difficulties in Coordination

In the same way as the girls have difficulty in integrating their sensory impressions (the information from the outer world), they may also have difficulty in coordinating their actions (their response to the outer world).

This difficulty can manifest itself in many ways. Individuals with Rett syndrome have difficulty in coordinating their active intake of information from the outer world (their "input") with their active performance in the outer world (their "output") — they do not respond as immediately as we do. For them it is also much more difficult to coordinate two kinds of outward actions concurrently, namely to "do two things at the same time" (output-output).

Not all the girls have equally severe problems and their ways of handling these problems may vary, but to more than half the girls these difficulties in coordination are very troublesome and hamper them a great deal.

Delayed Responses

Girls with Rett syndrome do one thing at a time. Furthermore, when they do something their motives are often unclear to us because they may act after a very long time-lag. Many people describe these girls as having a "slow reaction-time." It may take them a long time before they respond to a stimulus, regardless of whether this stimulus is a sensory impression, a verbal request, or a decision-of their own, and regardless of whether the response is a sound, a movement, or active exploration with the eyes. During the lapse between stimulus and response, the girls pull themselves together but their concentration rarely looks like concentration in the conventional sense of the word.

Hand-Eye Coordination

It is always difficult for the girls to perform actively; partly due to their apraxia, and partly because their acting is almost always preceded by their receiving and interpreting some kind of information to which their acting is a response. In novel or trying situations, it is almost impossible for these girls to receive a stimulus and to respond to it at once. The connection between input and output is not immediate.

Grasping, for instance, is a problem for these girls because they do not know how to do it. But it is also difficult for them since their hand-eye coordination is so poor. Looking (input) and grasping (output) at the same time is sometimes impossible. The girls have to take one thing at a time — first looking, then grasping. They often take a rapid glance at the object, look away, and then put out their hand and touch or grab the object without looking. This is a general description. The reality is often far more complex and complicated. If, for instance, a girl catches sight of a doll she has never seen before, she may make several rapid glances towards it and finally get so interested that she wants to try to grasp it. When she has made her decision, she is not able to reach for the doll at once, but has to prepare herself and force her body to perform the movement. This process may sometimes look like self-absorption. Sometimes instead, the girl's activity level is raised. If she is standing up she may begin to move her feet or bend forwards. If she is sitting down, she may rock or tense her body. She may start hyperventilating, teeth-grinding or making grimaces. Her hand stereotypies are intensified and she may have to extend an arm up in the air. Some girls look in all directions except towards the doll in question. Others, on the other hand, fix their eyes on the doll but may shut or screw up their eyes now and then. This spell of concentration may last for so long that onlookers tire or forget what the girl is up to. Commonly it lasts a few minutes. Then there is a sudden lunge, the girl's hand reaches out, hitting the doll. Sometimes she succeeds in grasping it, but often she fails and the doll flies away, landing somewhere out of her reach. When the hand is moving the eyes are turned away.

In this example, the girl demonstrates her various problems to us: she has difficulty in directly approaching a new object, and an inability to act directly and correctly in spite of will and desire (apraxia). There is also a long delay before the final action and the agitated concentration preceding it, and a poor ability to adjust the strength of the movement (as in the example, this often results in a reaction that is too sudden and too strong — the alternative is often no reaction at all; the girl pulls herself together, concentrates and exerts herself, but the hand does not make any directed movement whatsoever). Finally, she demonstrates a lack of hand-eye coordination.

OBSERVE KATHY FOR THIS

If you know, you can see it. An uninitiated or casual observer may not have noticed when the girl's sequence of actions began, but might have interpreted her deep concentration as a lack of interest. The movements towards the doll may have been interpreted as random motion, just one movement among all the others. The observer may not have realized what a very long time the girl needs in order to act, but on the contrary may have thought that she is a very quick actor judging by the suddenness of the movement she makes.

Similarly, one may see how a girl, when confronted with an obstacle on the floor — a doorstep or suchlike — takes a rapid glance at it, concentrates for a while, and then all of a sudden almost throws herself over the obstacle without looking where she is going.

MAT AT THE DOOR!

Coordination is improved by practice. When the object in question is a familiar one, when the girl has learned the movement, or work more smoothly. The eye and hand movements will be better coordinated and her period of concentration will not be so lengthy and agitated.

Over the years the girl's mobility decreases, and so does her motoric speed. All movements are slowed down. Then she will "catch up" better; the hand will reach an object without the eyes turning away. The response delay is still there, but it fits the girl's general slowness more naturally.

Other Kinds of Input-Output Coordination

It is not very hard to understand that people with Rett syndrome have difficulty in situations requiring a sequence of actions. It is harder to appreciate their profound inability to do two things concurrently even in a more general context. One little girl, for instance, happily watched her preschool peers painting pictures. She was very interested and her attention was very active. Noticing how amused she was, the staff wanted to give her a chance to participate. They dressed her in an apron, put a brush in her hand, and helped her to move it over the paper. They only wanted to help her, but the girl did not see it that way — she became unhappy and angry and gave such full expression to her feelings that she had to be taken into another room to calm down.

The girl could not manage to watch actively and paint actively at the same time. She had to choose, and she really wanted to watch her peers. When the adults tried to help her to paint they interfered with her watching and taking in the entertaining situation, and of course she objected to that. Maybe this girl will have to watch the other children painting once a day for many weeks in order to become so familiar with the situation that she later on might do something more than just look.

Another example is of a little girl who is looking at her pre-school peers singing and making movements to the music. She looks and she laughs and she is very fascinated. The aide wants to help her to have even more fun. She helps the girl down to the floor and starts moving her arms according to the rules of the game. But now the girl is no longer amused. She screams and cries and bites her hands. In this situation the girl could not manage to look actively and to act outwards at the same time. In addition, she had to take in the information given by the adult touching and moving her body. She had no chance to complete what she had begun—watching her peers playing. Probably the whole situation was chaotic to her.

A little later that day the same girl is dancing in a ring with the other children. An adult is holding one hand; a child the other. The girl is used to people holding her hands and does not mind or think about it. She has only to walk and she is certainly capable of doing that. It is fun to go round and round and it is not difficult because the others are leading, her legs move automatically. She has scope for active watching at the same time. She laughs and she really enjoys herself.

From an observer's point of view this girl's behavior may seem inconsistent — "sometimes she wants to participate and sometimes she does not." Of course some of her reactions can be explained by the different circumstances — there may have been a change in her emotional and mental energy, and she may have been in different moods. But basically her different reactions are due to the two situations actually differing in difficulty for her, despite appearing so alike.

The Degree of Active Effort is Crucial

The degree of the girls' difficulties in taking in information and at the same time acting outwards depends on the degree of activity demanded by each one of those operations. If the actions compete with each other with respect to the degree of attention needed, the girls will have to choose. They can only direct their attention actively to one thing at a time. When one of the actions is sufficiently familiar, or carried out automatically, it is possible for the girls to apply themselves also to something that demands more active attention. Everything works better when it has been carefully learned, or when the girls have been active for a while. This is also the reason why their stereotypies, which are highly automated movements, can, without difficulty, occur simultaneously with almost any other behavior. Only when something calls for a totally active effort from the girl, even the stereotypies will become a "disturbance" and accordingly cease.

These difficulties in coordination can also be made use of when a patient cries inconsolably and no conventional endeavors to console her have worked. This situation is not unusual and it is extremely upsetting for the girl and to those around her. Then a solution might be to divert the crying by offering her a stimulus with so large an impact that there is no "scope" for anything else. Many parents have discovered that a run in the car or a complete change of setting (like a visit to a neighbor) may quieten the crying and make the girl respond to the new situation with laughter or tranquil contentment. As for my own student, who is very fascinated by lights, it was helpful to move her into a totally dark room with a single candle burning. Of course, the type of stimulus that will call up the most positive attention and accordingly work best in these situations depends entirely on the individual girl.

Output-Output Coordination

In much the same way as it can be a problem to coordinate input and output, it can be equally difficult to coordinate two different types of output; that is, two kinds of outward actions.

This is true for all of us, but these girls are less skilled than we are, and less experienced. Thus, more actions are new or difficult to them, and they have a smaller repertoire of automatic movements. Their settings may seem uncomplicated and the demands made on them may seem simple, but the those with Rett syndrome are still engaged in solving problems during a larger part of the day than we are, in spite of our more complex lives. We still have more time to spare. But we, too, find it impossible to do two difficult things at the same time, or to simultaneously solve two problems. For example, most of us would find it extremely trying to do a difficult jigsaw puzzle and at the same time solve a mathematical problem. To act socially while at the same time concentrating on something complicated is as difficult for us as it is for these girls — many of us, for example, would not be able to talk while doing patterned knitting. To these girls, much easier tasks present exactly the same problems. Concentrating on grasping and at the same time trying to "talk" is quite impossible. Their only chance to grasp and "talk" simultaneously is when one of these actions is done without effort, "by itself." Otherwise each action will engage the girls totally.

The Girls Always Take In More Than They Are Able To Give Out

Since they often are forced to choose, because of apraxia, poor coordination, and limited environmental opportunities, it is easier for girls with Rett syndrome to take in than to give out, and consequently they devote more of their time to absorbing information than to transforming this information into practical action. Their input is always greater than their output. Even if we are uncertain of how much these girls understand, they do understand quite a lot. This is shown, for instance, by the little girl who starts crying when her siblings are talking about her with contempt, or by another little girl who always gets seizures when it is time to go to the doctor, even though no one has mentioned the crucial word. However, it often seems as if the girls do not understand at all — they seem self-absorbed and do not react to any information given in a particular situation.

Much later, it may become apparent that they have in fact taken in and remembered what has happened — they show that they recognize something, they repeat in words or by acting out something that they have been confronted with. For instance, one mother recalls how a physical therapist had come to see her daughter, who had not previously had any regular physical therapy. On a later occasion the therapist told the rest of the staff and demonstrated to them how she had worked with the girl, who was present on this occasion and showed with all her behavior that she remembered the situation and understood that the physical therapist was describing the situation and her in it.

Sometimes you might ask a girl to do something you are sure she understands and is able to manage, you ask and nag but she does not respond. Finally you give up, concluding that she is not responsive just now — and when you turn your back on her she does what you asked for, as if there was nothing to it! She did know what it was all about.

Through such examples, the girls show that they take in and process and understand, but even more often we do not get any confirmation at all. It is important then that we — who are so busy talking and acting all the time — do not forget that action in itself is not the entire skill, and that absence of action does not necessarily mean absence of knowledge.

KEY POINT

6 Mental Retardation

In the parents' accounts there is no such convincing evidence of mental regression as there is of a decline in other areas. While girls with Rett syndrome visibly lose their previous fine motor, verbal, and social skills, they seem rather to come to a standstill in mental development. The girls also seem to stay at the same intellectual level in the future; that is, there does not seem to be any further development to higher levels of abstraction. Even if they acquire more and more experiences, they do not utilize these experiences in a more advanced manner.

As the girls grow older, their mental handicap becomes more and more evident. They do not perform as can be expected from their biological age. The behavior and reasoning which we see are those normally shown by a child under 2 years of age. Of course, girls with Rett syndrome differ in this respect too, but generally they behave in a way normal for children of about 18 months of age. Actually, the girls' development has generally advanced rather normally up to the age of 18 months.

FAMILIARITY
STRUCTURE
MORE EXPERIENCE
↓
BETTER UNDERSTAND
AND PERFORM

Concrete and Tangible Experiences

Girls with Rett syndromes' comprehension of the world is dependent on their own concrete and tangible experiences. They understand by associating and recognizing. The more familiar and structured a situation, that is, the more experience they have had of the situation, the better the girls will understand and the better they will perform. Only when situations are very much alike or contain the same emotionally charged details, or when the knowledge learned is strongly emotive, can the girls carry over the knowledge from a familiar situation and adjust and use this knowledge in a new situation.

For example, in an eating situation, regardless of which room and table is used and which adult is feeding her, one little girl always acts in the same way — she touches the adult's arm to show that she wants another spoonful — but she very seldom displays this behavior in other situations where it would be appropriate to use this same gesture to express a desire for something else.

Another example is when the transfer of knowledge to new situations will have negative consequences. One little girl had been frightened by a stay in hospital and later identified all people in white coats as dangerous people. When her mother wanted to take her to a bakery shop the girl refused to go inside, because the sales clerk was wearing a white coat. This example demonstrates, on the one hand, how well-learned and generalized the knowledge is, but, on the other, how limited the girl's understanding actually is.

The girls take in new situations/people/settings by a quick glance, selecting some details which they later explore closely and carefully with their eyes and other senses. (It is not certain that the girls choose the details we would consider the most logical.) These details are then associated, individually or patterned together, with the situation/people/setting in question, and in this way the girls learn and remember for future reference. The ability to recognize and remember is greater the more motivated the girls are, the more important the situation is to them, and the more times they have been confronted with it.

CONSISTENCY

Understanding Language

All of the girls understand the meaning of some learned words and associate them with specific objects and situations. Many girls can also follow simple directions and understand simple information which does not necessarily have to be learned but has to be understandable to and motivating for the girls in some way. It must fit into their frame of reference and their system of values.

It is very difficult to decide whether the girls also have a more extensive word comprehension—this is a question which deeply puzzles those in contact with them. Nearly everybody agrees that they understand more than they are given credit for and that this understanding can sometimes be almost complete, but no one dares to decide whether this is actually a verbal understanding or if the understanding is more intuitive. I find this very hard to judge; partly due to the girls' difficulty in "proving" their word comprehension by talking, acting, and following directions; partly due to their displaying great variation in all areas of behavior. I have seen several instances, however, where the girls calm down when one suddenly "hits the mark" in trying to comfort them verbally, and many of them do show less anxiety if they are verbally prepared for what is about to happen. In my experience, many girls also have shown very adequate emotional reactions to something I or somebody else has said to them, though we have been talking in a rather "emotionally neutral" tone, and though the girl "ought not" to have understood. There are also many examples of how the girls laugh — or cry — "in the right places."

In this area, when we are dependent on intuition and interpretation, it can be easily appreciated that part of the girls' handicap is within ourselves.

Understanding Space

The girls can act rather easily in familiar settings: they know their way about the room, they know when the school bus is turning "their" way, they know where objects important to them are placed, what the objects represent, and what their function is. Many parents report how quickly their daughters learn to find their way in new surroundings and how well they can remember a place even if it has been years between their first and second visit there. They can walk directly into the right room and find the clock or the picture or whatever it was that fascinated them on their first visit.

On the other hand, in most cases it is quite inconceivable to allow them to be unattended out of doors, even in familiar settings. If they should wander off, they could not find their way back again. They are totally dependent on fixed marks in order to know where they are, and it is by no means certain that the things they have noticed during their walk will still be there and can function as marks on a later occasion, even if the girls should happen to turn in the right direction towards home.

Understanding Time

The girls' comprehension of time is generally very poor; a fact that creates *DRINK* difficulties for the girls as well as for their caregivers. Everything must *TIME* happen at once; they have little patience. In this case, too, they act on the basis of associations. Zip-suit=out, this means that as soon as the zip-suit is on one is to go outdoors, and it is very hard for the girl to wait inside until everybody else is dressed for going out as well. Depending on her personality, the girl may fall asleep, have a temper tantrum, or may no longer be interested in going out when it is finally time to do so.

LUNCH - BANGING IN TABLES

Likewise plate = food, and if the food is not immediately placed on her plate the girl may call attention to this in every possible way, like flailing her hand at the table, rocking her chair, screaming or sweeping her plate to the floor.

The girls' understanding of time is built completely on routines and symbols, and the more routines, the "better" their understanding.

ROUTINES ARE VITAL

As they grow older and gain more experiences, their patience develops — in situations repeated daily, the girls gradually learn that the things they look forward to actually will happen — even if they will have to wait for a while — and they no longer have to act so violently. Having a comprehension of time based on routines, however, also means that the girls may be unhappy and confused if the routines are broken.

Understanding Cause and Effect

In this concept formation, too, the girls use simple associations. They can associate the wall switch with the lamplight and the faucet with running water. But even if they understand what belongs to what and know what will happen, they do not realize the true meaning of what is happening. They do not know why it happens or how it really works. Here too, they are dependent on the situation and on routines. Together with a particular person and at a particular faucet one girl may be able to get the water to run whereas she is unable to do this with another person or at another faucet, despite the faucets differing only in color and not in any other respects.

The girls will learn by experience that "if I do this, that will happen." In familiar situations they can understand that they will be able to have an effect on their surroundings, for example, by looking at their glass when they want to drink or by walking up to the tape recorder when they want to have some music. The more attention they get from such actions the more often they will use them and in more situations. More complex causal relationships and sequences of thoughts like "if I first do this and then do that, that thing will probably happen and then that will be the result" seem to be beyond the capacity of these girls — at any rate it is difficult for them to make such thinking clear to us.

Understanding Quantity

When it comes to the girls' ability to compare different quantities, many parents and teachers are uncertain. These girls seldom find themselves in situations where they have reason to make comparisons regarding number and size, for instance. Some people have noticed, however, that they always want the biggest piece of the cake or apple or whatever, if they are given a choice between two pieces of different sizes. Some girls pick out the glass containing more liquid and want that glass to drink from. The parents describe how one girl carefully watches the glass being filled up and "crossly grumbles" if there is not as much in her glass as in those of her siblings.

Understanding Quality

The girls understand the function of familiar objects and can also see similarities between different objects and 'classify' them accordingly.

One girl knows that a door is a door and behind it there is something else—independently of how the door looks and opens. Many discern what is edible and put those things and only those into the mouth. One girl, who is very fond of clocks and watches, suddenly caught sight of my wristwatch when we were playing, and at once got very interested. She forgot the toy we had been playing with and instead carefully studied my watch—then she turned her head and looked at the aide's wristwatch as well (without any request from us) and looked from one watch to the other several times, and then smiled a little.

Another little girl knows that all cows are called "moo"—whether they are familiar to her or cows she has never met before, and whether they are real cows or cows in a picture.

Many girls show an incipient comprehension of symbols. They attribute some permanence to objects—they know that things continue to exist even though they cannot for the moment see or touch them. They search actively for things important to them, which they remember are to be found in a certain place. Many of the girls understand that a picture can represent a real object or a real event.

Understanding Pictures

Almost all the girls show great interest in pictures, photographs, and drawings, in black and white as well as in color, and also the moving pictures on TV. Many of the girls understand well-known pictures where they have learned the meaning of the picture by an association with a real object. Several girls can also interpret new and unfamiliar pictures if these show something the girls are acquainted with and interested in.

*COMMUNICA-
TION
BOARD*

It is not possible to say exactly how many of the girls have this ability. Since they were seldom actually screened for this ability, the answers varied a lot. Such a screening of girls with Rett syndrome would be of great interest in the future, even if suitable methods are difficult to find.

In 16 cases, however, the people close to the girls were entirely convinced that they really understood and interpreted even unfamiliar pictures. Only 6 of the girls were assumed not to read pictures at all. Of the remaining 17, the people interviewed thought that they did read pictures, but they could not say whether the girls also understood pictures in the sense of being able to interpret pictures unfamiliar to them. In many of those cases it was, however, stressed that the girls had a great interest in pictures — "greater than in toys" — and that they were able to show that they preferred some pictures to others and that they anyway reacted "in the right way" to familiar pictures.

When I visited the home of one of the girls, I tried to test her picture comprehension more systematically. In advance I had selected pictures I considered likely to be within this girl's sphere of interest. The pictures were color photographs sharply outlined and moderately detailed — neither too messy nor too schematic. I showed the pictures two at a time — within each pair fairly different pictures; for example, a cat and an eating situation — and I also shifted their relative positions so that their location would not influence the girl's choice. First, I talked a little about the pictures in a way designed to awaken the girl's interest ("here they all are seated round the table, eating, lots of food, soft drinks in the bottles; I wonder if they have filled their glasses yet" and then the girl glanced at that picture or "what a nice cat, I have a cat at home too, but she is dotted with many colors and this one is all black" and the girl at once looked at the picture of the cat).

Gradually I changed to more direct statements ("have you seen such a..." — "Oh look what an...") since the parents considered that this would not disturb her, and it did not. I tried to make my statements more indirect than demanding. Every time I talked about a picture the girl showed with a rapid glance that she was aware of which picture was in question. In all, about ten pictures were used, in many different combinations. In all but one case the girl looked at the correct picture. The exception was a picture of a girl swimming. This picture was preferred by the girl in three different combinations and independent of position. The girl always chose this picture, regardless of which picture I was talking about. She is very fond of swimming, and the water was a beautiful blue color which this girl often chooses in daily life. The girl was so captivated by the activity that her stereotypies almost entirely ceased. Now and then she became "aware" of me and of what was going on and would then start hyperventilating. This *CHOICES !* behavior immediately ceased, however — much to my own surprise I must admit — when I explained to her that this "picture thing" she could do or give up just as she pleased, the decision was hers, and she had all the time in the world. Then I continued to talk about the pictures, pretending I enjoyed doing it whether she looked or not, and soon she was participating again.

The girl used her eyes only, until we reached the last picture. Then she took her hand up from her lap and patted the picture, which was an advertisement showing a girl eating little jelly cars from a bag. I let that picture alone remain on the table and placed a real candy bag of the same sort beside it. The girl looked quickly several times from the picture to the candy bag and then moved her hand to the real bag. We opened the bag and she had some of the candies. I left the bag on the table with some jelly cars next to it, so she could attempt to take them. Grasping such small items is beyond the capacity of this girl, but she can pat on small items to signal that she wants them, which is in fact what she did. The picture remained on the table all the time, but it was no longer of any interest. When the girl's interest in the candy bag was at its highest and she had her hand lifted to smash it, I quickly put a scarf over the bag. The hand landed on the scarf, the girl looked and then she moved her hand away. She changed over to patting the picture of the candy bag instead. I took the scarf away, let the girl pat

OPTION FOR TEACHING SYMBOL ASSOC.

the candy bag for a while again, and then put the scarf back as before and the girl again changed over to patting the picture. Then I put the picture away. I waited until the girl was eagerly interested in the real candy bag again and then put the scarf over it. Now she insistently patted the scarf. She could not take it away herself, but she was very pleased when I did.

When I had previously presented a doll to the same girl she patted it, but not at all with the same interest. When I put a scarf over the doll the girl's patting totally ceased and she did not begin acting again when I took the scarf away.

The above account not only tells us about this girl's ability to interpret pictures; it also shows her verbal comprehension, her incipient comprehension of object permanence, and above all, it shows us how very important it is to take into consideration the girls' motivation and interests when trying to judge their abilities. I knew that this girl was fond of candies but it was a mere coincidence that I chose a bag of jellies — which happened to be the only picture of candy I could find. I was lucky because it turned out that jelly cars were her favorite candies. In comparison, this girl is not very fond of dolls, and the use of a doll could not get her to accomplish what she did with the candy bag.

Intellectual Level - Level of Functioning

As demonstrated above, it is very difficult to assess what a girl with Rett syndrome can or cannot do, and what she does and does not understand. It is easy to judge a girl as a "complete mental drop-out" when she sits there inactive and apathetic with a dull expression on her face, not reacting at all when spoken to or when one tries to stimulate her. But when you see the same girl on a different occasion or in a different setting, leaning over a picture of a baby and with a face full of life and joy saying "be-be", it is no longer that easy.

In view of the knowledge and experience we have today, girls with Rett syndrome are severely mentally retarded. Using Piaget's theory, the girls' performance as a whole can hardly be placed higher than stage 4 on the "sensorimotor intelligence" scale [Olsson & Rett, 1985].

One must, however, consider that Piaget in his theory uses to a large extent external motor activities as evidence of internal mental operations. Due to their various handicaps, these girls have great difficulty in motoric acting. They may also show some unevenness in their mental development. Some of them who in no way show any comprehension of object permanence can still display a clear understanding of symbols by reading and interpreting unfamiliar pictures. This means that in this respect they have progressed further and are in transition from sensorimotor intelligence to pre-operational intelligence. I have not seen any girl whom I with any certainty have been able to place higher in the scale than on that transition stage. There are some, however, who remain at an earlier level of development than stage 4 in the Piaget scale.

Due to various obstacles within themselves and with their environment, these girls, however, rarely function at their optimal level. They have a disorder which affects their physical and their mental development. Other handicaps also prevent them from fully participating in, understanding, and influencing their environment, and thus deprive them of experiences important to intellectual development. As a result, their intellectual level will not be consistent, but their capacity will be greatest within those areas where they have had the opportunity to obtain the most experience.

Consequently the girls cannot always, if ever, make use of the intellectual resources that they actually have. This means that their intellectual level is not necessarily the same as or reflected by their functioning level.

If neither we nor the girls can "get hold of" the appropriate resources it may seem better not to persist in trying, yet sometimes it can be important to have a more precise definition of the intellectual possibilities of a particular girl. This could be necessary, for instance, in order to give her a more appropriate treatment, with demands and aids adjusted to her needs, conducive to bridge the gap between her intellectual level and her level of functioning. To help her in this way we have to know what in her behavior is the result of what. The methods we have today for screening intelligence are not, however, very suited to these individuals and do not do them full justice. An important aim in future research on Rett syndrome would be to create methods facilitating more systematic and genuine information on the intellectual potentials of this group.

7   Communication Disorders

Will of Contact — Capacity for Contact

When asked how their daughters behaved as infants, most of the parents answered that they were "nice and quiet," — "easy and satisfied with life" and "without any demands." The girls could, for instance, lie awake in bed for a long while, quiet and not calling for attention. "It was I who had to see to it that she got fed, she did not cry for it," said several mothers. While many parents feel that they had a normal contact with their infant, others claim that there were some deviations in contact right from the beginning. By analyzing the parents' accounts more thoroughly, one can see that the girls have often been markedly inactive, and that this often goes for their contact as well. They have been inferior to other children in taking initiatives and have not, like other infants, been able to show that they long for human contact. In addition, their responses to their parents' contacts often have been inert and feeble. Even if they accepted the contact and showed by their facial expression and bodily relaxation that they appreciated it, they still did not display the same eagerness and enthusiasm in their responses as did other infants, but were more listless and less persistent. Only rarely could they imitate (wave or clap their hands for instance) as early as their siblings, and they seldom actively participated in peek-a-boo games even if they enjoyed them.

About one-third of the parents pointed out that the girls' babbling had been deviant, in the sense that they babbled less often, less lively, and with less variety than other children or siblings of the same age.

The deviations of contact ability are mostly minor and they do not involve all the girls. Even if there have been a few cases of more pronounced lack of interest, these girls have never been markedly negative to interpersonal contacts in the way often associated with autistic infants. None of the parents described themselves as rejected by their daughters; on the contrary, all of them felt that they had had good emotional contact with their infant girl.

It is natural to have different expectations and demands of an infant in its cradle than of a child who is beginning to make words and move around. Even if the child's inability for contact does not in itself change, it will become more and more evident the older the child grows. This, however, does not sufficiently explain the change in the girls' contact behavior. Most parents do witness a dramatic deterioration in their contacts with their daughters, when they are somewhere between the age of 1 and 3 years. At this age there is a period when it becomes harder to make contact with them and they appear more withdrawn, and at the same time show a more marked lack of interest and, on the whole, a diminishing participation in their external world. Most parents do not agree that this withdrawal was autistic in that it was impossible to break through, or that the girl did not want to have contact. The withdrawal was not that profound or complete, they say. Many parents explain this withdrawal by assuming that their daughter has been so preoccupied by the progress of her disorder and the resulting problems that she simply has no capacity, time or strength left for the external world. Most parents claim that even if their daughter did not respond in the expected way, they never entirely lost their contact with her — but they sometimes had to try hard not to.

Gradually, the children come out of this stage and are again able to take a greater interest in their surroundings. Some parents work very closely with their daughters to reestablish a more normal relationship. In other cases the girls come out of their isolation without such great efforts.

As time goes on, contact with and interest in the surrounding environment continues to improve. When asked what has changed and improved in the course of the disorder, most people answer that the contact with the girl is now better. This fact is especially emphasized regarding the younger girls, where it is of immediate interest, since the girl has just left or is just coming out of the most trying phase of the disorder. Within all age groups, however, this *is* reported as the greatest improvement. Surely this is evidence of a continuously improving contact ability, but also, I assume, of the fact that the girls have become more "at home" in their lives and then have more time left to make use of their improved ability. When one experiences a better emotional contact with a girl this is certainly also a result of a higher sensitivity towards her and a better interpretation of her different ways of communicating.

I also think that this emphasis on improved social and emotional interaction says something about how utterly painful it is for us not to be able to experience an immediate contact with another human being, without having to initially overcome a lot of obstacles. When asked what is most difficult and what they would do first to ameliorate, if it were possible, the predominating answer from the people interviewed is that the difficulty most acutely felt is not being able to understand what the girl wants or how she feels, and how to behave to help her — and they wish that they could find a way to better interpret her feelings, desires, and needs.

Rett Syndrome — Infantile Autism

Even if persons with Rett syndrome have periods and moments of isolation they differ from autistic children in many ways when it comes to contact with the outside world. The choice is not between dead objects and living persons, but rather between a complete presence and a complete withdrawal. When the girls are withdrawn they are turned inwards on themselves and do not care for either objects or people. When they are "present" they are open to and interested in objects as well as people — even if they can only concentrate on one at a time.

In addition, the girls almost always prefer people to objects. Unlike autistic children, they do not use objects to "shield themselves" from human contacts. They also prefer the company of people to solitude. In a safe and familiar setting they actually appreciate being the center of attention and may object if they are not. Several parents even report epileptic seizures triggered off when the girls feel overlooked in such circumstances.

Unlike autistic children, those with Rett syndrome have good eye contact. Sometimes, however, they may demonstrate a lack of interest by avoiding eye contact. They may also begin to make contact with a new person by a series of rapid glances, but when they are sympathetically interested and the contact is established, they fix their gaze and look long and hard and with joy into the eyes of the other person.

Then they also want to look very closely just like when they look at objects and pictures. The girls respond with a smile to people they know or take a fancy to — even if the smile, like so many of their reactions, may be very delayed.

Generally the girls are very fond of bodily contact; cuddling as well as rough and tough play. They keep their distance and show a normal reserve with people they do not know. All the girls in the study can show that they have their favorites and that there are people they do not care for or actually dislike. However, they make and respond to social contacts on their own terms. All of the girls studied are able to take the initiative in making interpersonal contacts, but their methods of doing so vary greatly depending upon the degree of their physical handicap. For instance, one girl, who is wheelchair bound, can look alternately from her father to the sofa in the living room to show that she wants to rest there with him, one of their daily rituals. On the other hand, another girl, who is ambulatory, can walk up to and place herself with her back towards the person in whose lap she wants to sit. Each girl has her own individual signals. If one knows the signals they are clear enough — if one does not, they may be almost impossible to observe and interpret to people who are used to another kind of language.

Though the girls sometimes seem uninterested or even withdrawn they still have a high "degree of presence." They have difficulty in conveying what they themselves want and feel, nevertheless they are tremendously clever at catching the atmosphere and reading other people's tone of voice and body language. "It is impossible to play false with her," many people say. "If you are unhappy or anxious or angry she knows it very well, however much you try to hide it." This ability demonstrates that the girls actually are turned towards the outside world, even when it does not seem so.

They demonstrate their interest in other people in many other ways as well. Most of them scrutinize the people in a new place before they study the room and the things in the room. While they have difficulty in following objects with their eyes, the girls generally have no such difficulties with people. Those who are interested in pictures or TV prefer, with few exceptions, pictures of people; especially children. Many parents report that their daughters particularly like children, and are very fond of watching children play.

They often prefer songs to instrumental music, especially children singing, and they like live music better than radio or tapes, if they have a choice. The girls recognize different voices, and even those who do not show that they recognize any other sounds, are able to read voices and, without using their eyes, associate them with the right person.

8   Communication

Though the girls have an emotional interest in and a desire for social contact, their capacity for contact is not a "normal" one. They do not have the ability to express their wish for contact in a conventional manner. They also have difficulty in conveying more direct messages, wishes, and will, but mostly this too is due to a lack of capacity rather than a lack of interest.

Furthermore, part of their handicap is caused by those of us who form their outer world. We are not used to conscious and varied analysis and interpretation of nonverbal signals. Although we do know that these children are handicapped, it is often very hard for us to put this knowledge into practice. If, in an eating situation, a little girl lifts her hand and pats a piece of bread we at once interpret this as a wish for a sandwich. If the same girl walks up to the livingroom shelf and knocks some records onto the floor it is easy to forget her limited means of expression and act as if she were just an ordinary child. We say "naughty, naughty, don't touch" and put the records back higher up on the shelf, beyond her reach — and we forget to reflect on *why* the girl knocked down the records. Maybe she wanted to listen to some music? Actually her behavior is just the same as at the dining table, and this is the limit of her performance ability. She is not able to take a record and hand it to the adult. Neither can she use words or sounds to ask for what she wants. But after all we do know that the girl never touches anything without really being interested in that object. She is able to make a choice and she has chosen the records in the only way she can.

In addition, our pace differs from theirs, and the girls with their slower pace do not always succeed in making it clear to us that they are trying to tell us something. Furthermore, we do not always have the time to apply different interpretations of their behavior. Nor are the girls always ready to respond to *our* efforts at communication. Perhaps this is sometimes due to the fact that we, here too, expect them to communicate on our terms, and forget what their terms actually are, and in which sphere of interest they are situated.

One example is the little girl busy playing with her doll. She grabs it, bangs it to the floor, looks, and listens. She is very interested and the play is complex and calls for her full attention. In spite of her handicaps she is now busy listening, looking and feeling (input) as well as grabbing and banging the doll (output) and probably also observing the connection between her own movements and the resulting sounds (coordination). In addition, she is keenly babbling. Now her mother calls her to come. She calls "come" and the girl's name many times, but nothing happens; that is, the child goes on playing. It is not that she does not hear, the words probably come in all right — but they disappear somewhere on their way and they do not result in her making any outer response. Then the mother, supported by her knowledge of her daughter's preferences, decides to compete for her attention. She will offer a stimulus which is "stronger" to the child than her play with the doll. "Come for an ice cream," she calls out. Then the girl stops her play and listens. Her mother repeats the offer and the child lets her doll go and crawls off to the kitchen. Had her mother, however, entered the room with a tooth-brush in her hand instead, telling her daughter that it was time to brush her teeth — something she really dislikes — she may have intensified her play with the doll instead, completely ignoring her mother. To a casual observer these three situations may seem very similar to each other, but this girl does interact with her environment and responds to it with varying reactions in each of the three cases.

Even if individuals with Rett syndrome are turned towards the outer world and do have a desire for communication, they have a rather small repertoire of means from which to choose. They do not have so many ways to express themselves, and their signals are often limited in strength and duration. How long they will persist with their

DURATION OF COMMUNICATION EFFORT DEPENDS ON :
① PREVIOUS EXPERIENCES
② POSSIBILITIES IN PRESENT SITUATION
③ IMPORTANCE OF MESSAGE TO BE CONVEYED

efforts depends on their previous experiences and the possibilities in the present situation — and of course also on how important it is to them to convey to us the message in question.

Sometimes it will end happily, as in this example. A little girl is eating her lunch. She likes it and demonstrates her eagerness with her whole body, opening her mouth wide and leaning towards the spoon. After some time, however, she suddenly refuses the food. Through her behavior she demonstrates that she wants food, but when the spoon arrives she closes her mouth and compresses her lips. When the spoon disappears she is unhappy, but she still will not accept the food when another spoonful is offered. Her teacher tries other options — salad, bread, water to drink — but no, the child wants the macaroni pudding. Finally she starts crying. Then her teacher serves her a fresh helping of pudding, digging deep into the dish to get it hot. Now she eats — her whole helping! The problem was that the food on her plate was cold. She wanted food — but she wanted it hot. In this case the child was as clear as she could be, and she persisted in her rather simple message, so that it was at last possible for us to make a correct interpretation. Besides, we were two adults fully concentrated on one person and we could help one another to guess; the room was quiet with no other people there, and we were not pressed for time. So much may sometimes be necessary in order to satisfy a simple wish!

Our Role in Communication

At other times the end is not completely happy. We cannot get confirmation of the correctness of our interpretations, or we cannot fulfill the girls' requirements. On the same afternoon I went with the child just described and her mother as they left the day care center. When we got to their home the mother wished to give her little daughter pleasure by playing a tape for her. But she was not at all pleased and even refused to go into the living room. She remained standing in the hallway, looking at the outer door. Then she looked at her mother. She began to walk towards the room but then returned to the door. She became more and more agitated, breathing hard and wringing her hands. Finally she began to cry unhappily. At first I wondered if this situation was caused by my being there, but I did not get the feeling that I was at all involved—the girl neither payed any attention to me nor did she ignore me in any suspicious way. Her mother also thought that this had nothing to do with me. She pondered and puzzled and finally thought she had found the explanation.

Their usual routine was to go shopping before they went home, and *Routine* today we had gone straight home from the daycare center. Of course, this was a mistake in the eyes of the girl — she had missed something she was used to and also liked very much. Now it was too late to change the procedure, but her mother spoke to her in a very nice way. She told her daughter that she understood that she was upset and that she knew why. And eventually the child was persuaded to go into the living room and listen to the music.

Expressing Needs and Wants

Every girl in the study can show her pleasure and displeasure by emotional expressions, body language, and facial expression. Most of them are also able to express "don't want to" in a manner understandable to their surroundings. How they express this is to some extent dependent on the response they get. If, for example, a girl has made up her mind not to take part in physiotherapy she may begin showing this by offering resistance, avoiding eye contact with the person performing the therapy. If the adult cannot motivate her to participate, but still carries on with the therapy, the girl may become angry or begin to cry. If this still does not help she may resort to falling asleep. If this situation is repeated many times it may result in her falling asleep whenever it is time for physiotherapy.

Almost all the girls in the study can show that they want food when they are seated at the dining table with the food in view. But it is much harder for them to show their needs and wants, when anticipating a situation, in any way other than by mere emotional expressions. For instance only one-third of the girls manage to express hunger in a more advanced way. Walking up to the refrigerator door, looking persistently from the stove to the mother, clapping a picture of a plate are different examples of how the girls are able to express themselves.

Almost one-half of them can show their wishes in a more modulated way, but in most cases in only a very few situations. For instance, many close their mouth to the spoon and then look firmly at the glass to indicate that they want to drink instead. Some of them can look from the TV set to the adult to show that they want to look at something on the television. Others can place themselves next to their stroller or pat their outerwear to express their wish for a walk. In most cases these expressions of need and will have to be interpreted by someone who knows her very well. To other people the signals can easily be concealed by other behaviors, which may be just as striking.

KEY

✶ None of the girls has the capacity for expressing herself in a way so general and at the same time so distinct that anybody would understand her.

Capacity for Verbal Expression

Even if many of the girls were vocalizing less than their siblings, most of them have learned some words and also begun to use them in an appropriate manner. The younger ones continue to use words, but very seldom. Many often articulate a word when exhaling during hyperventilation, a fact which makes it very difficult for those around them to understand that a word really was said. Many parents describe this way of talking as "she whispers." For some girls it seems easier to get a word out if it is surrounded by other sounds, which makes it easy to overlook that word and assume the whole utterance has just been another string of babbles. Some vocalize and babble frequently and vividly, but without words and meaning and without the intention of communication.

KATHY! EXPRESSES EMOTION WITH VOCALS

    On the whole, sounds and babble are seldom used for communication, but more as an expression of feelings, or as an accompaniment to play. The girls sometimes use words to name pictures and objects. But generally it seems as if they most often use their words in a random manner. When they really do want to express themselves to those around them their verbal apraxia becomes apparent. Like many other people, I too have witnessed how these girls want to and try to talk but do not succeed. Some exert themselves to the utmost, work with their whole body, make a lot of mouth movements, and at the same time concentrate intensely on the person they want to convey their message to.

In spite of this — or just because of their great efforts — they do not succeed in producing any words. "It is as if the words are on the tip of her tongue, but she cannot get them out" many people say. When the girls do not try at all, the words may come almost "by themselves." Many can call "mama" in moments of panic. In moments of harmony and relaxation the words may come like a sudden breakthrough. This does not happen many times in a girl's life, but it may happen some time in the life of many girls. For example, one girl was downtown once with her father and became very fascinated by the traffic lights. While they waited for the green man her father talked and told her all about the lights and what the red man meant. That same evening at the dining table the child suddenly said "red man" in a clear voice. In another case the grandfather was staying with the family for a while. When he came downstairs one morning and said "good morning" the girl answered "hi, grandpa" in a distinct voice — and this is something which is far beyond her usual capacity.

Some parents report that their daughters "perform better" when they are asleep — that they vocalize a lot more and produce more word-like sounds in a manner they are not capable of when awake. This information was given spontaneously in the course of my study, but it would be very interesting to investigate these facts in a more systematic way. Eight such instances were mentioned. Another two girls vocalize more often and in a more word-like way when they are "tired or about to fall asleep."

Many parents also report how in connection with an epileptic seizure their daughters can be more "talkative," and perform better both mentally and physically.

The older children are, in general, quieter than the younger ones. They also have more feeble signals and they are not so persistent in their attempts to communicate. "It was as if she really wanted to talk," one mother said, "and then she could not and she was unable to and finally she gave it up and now she hardly tries at all."

Other Modes of Expression

When their motor ability allows it, those with Rett syndrome can of course express their will by moving or touching (as, for example, the little girl who walked up to her outerwear and patted it to announce that she wanted to go for a walk). Eye-pointing, however, is the predominant method of expressing a wish. Eye-pointing means that a person looks at something she wants to do or get (or at a picture representing the desired item or situation). For example, there is one girl who, when she is out for a walk with her parents, can show where she wants her wheelchair to go by firmly staring in that direction. Another example is looking at something particularly desirable on the dining table. Often a girl looks from the adult to the thing she wants and back again, repeatedly until the adult has understood the message. Two thirds of the girls, from all age groups, do eye-pointing.

Others seek information through their eyes in other ways, by "asking," for instance. One little girl at once observed that the fan in the barn had been removed and looked from her mother to the empty wall until she got an explanation from her mother. A very common *OBSERVE* situation is when a girl gives a stranger a quick glance, then looks at *KATHY FOR* her mother, who is to acknowledge and introduce this stranger — and *THIS* only then does the girl begin to study the new person more thoroughly.

This ability to use the eyes to give and request information is very pronounced in many of the individuals studied. In others it is more feeble and difficult to interpret, sometimes depending on their technique (very *PAY* short and quick glances) and sometimes perhaps on the fact that one does *ATTENTION!* not expect their signals and consequently does not notice them.

The ability to eye-point does not fall off with increasing age or with the progress of the disorder. On the contrary, it often becomes better and also will be used for communication purposes. The eyes will often be more firmly fixed and the glances easier for those around to observe. Even when a girl is physically and mentally "down" and no other means of communication will work, the eye-pointing remains stable.

When talking about those who are not described as "eye-pointers," many still consider them to be "talking with their eyes." They express their feelings and moods through their eyes, and even those who otherwise have a very small repertoire of behaviors often do have very expressive eyes.

Indirect Signals

The girls also express themselves in other ways which may not be conscious communication, but which still may serve as signals to us, giving us information. The intensity of their stereotypies and the girls' general level of activity are examples of such signals.

The degree of self-absorption is another example. If a girl "turns off," this may be caused by physical or mental factors, or she may be so preoccupied with another activity that she has no scope to spare. Her withdrawal may also be a more direct signal to us, announcing that she does not want to participate, that she finds something too difficult, too foolish, too boring, or that she cannot manage to concentrate any longer. Most people are able to object or walk away from situations like these, but if one cannot do that, there is not much choice — the individual with Rett syndrome can cry or scream or "turn off," or even fall asleep, should this be necessary.

When one has a small repertoire with only a few responses and signals, each behavior has to represent many things. If a girl has "turned off," the proper interpretation might sometimes be: "This is a bore — I cannot amuse myself and I am really sick of this view. If nobody helps me to move my wheelchair in another direction, I have no other choice but to withdraw into myself."

The people who know the girl generally know when she really needs to be left alone and when she needs help to come out of her withdrawal.

9   Emotional Channels

To individuals with Rett syndrome the clash between conscious thought and unconscious feeling gives rise to many problems. In these girls feeling will always win; that is, it is their deepest feelings that will occasionally induce them to overcome their difficulties and perform in spite of their "inability." Using emotional channels, feelings, instead of thoughts, the intellectual channels, means more than just being motivated. One has to be emotionally motivated. Girls with Rett syndrome take in what they like and what has meaning and value to them, and it is the same things that can induce them to act.

The girls perform at their maximum in situations which are meaningful to them and where they can participate without "observing" themselves and their own acting. As soon as they begin to think about what they are doing, the risk of being blocked will increase. "To think" and "to do" counteract each other and provide another type of coordination difficulty. Since they do not consciously know how to use their bodies, the conscious mental effort seems to disturb, rather than facilitate, their motor movements. Trying to intellectually motivate these girls will consequently not work, but will rather impede their acting, since it will make the process conscious to them. There is also a risk of making them conscious of what they are doing by encouragement as well as by demands. This does not mean that one should not ask and encourage the girls to act — but it will probably be better to direct their attention to the object of their desire rather than to themselves. Instead of saying "yes, try and take it!" it may work better to say "yes, it is really a nice (object)." Nevertheless, in daily life one often says just "take it" if a girl is about to grasp something. If the words and the situation are repeated a sufficient number of times and she succeeds in understanding and performing what she should, these words, too, will later serve as a help to her. The words will be associated with the situation as a whole and work as an aid and a signal to the girl, so that she will know what to do, and they will also stimulate her to set off acting. Praising these girls too enthusiastically may make them so conscious of their acting that a repetition of the action in question will be prevented or impeded.

But their mental operations are not only governed from without. Often, their own efforts also make them aware of and directed towards themselves and their acting. They may be totally blocked, and then they will not be able to perform what they most want to do. The little girl standing by the tricycle, for instance, did not succeed in performing any directed movement at all, but all her great efforts ended up in nothing. When a girl's feelings carry her directly towards the goal, or when her conscious efforts are slackened, her potential to obtain what she wants will increase. In other circumstances, the same little girl, without thinking, might have walked up to the tricycle and at least put her hand on the handlebars and lifted her foot to the pedal. "Without thinking" really means not to think, and actually helps the girl to achieve her goal.

Should one ask a girl to say "hi" or plainly demonstrate that one expects her to respond to one's own "hello," one can be fairly sure that she will say nothing at all. But if one should just say "hello" without addressing any particular person, one should not be surprised if the girl sometimes will answer with a "hi."

Here is a further example. I am having dinner with a family. The girl has a soft drink in her glass and I ask the mother how she likes it being carbonated. "Well," the mother says, "maybe she likes juice better." — "Noo," says the daughter promptly. "Oh, your mother is wrong," says the mother and laughs. "Yes," says the daughter, laughing back at her mother. Now of course we all laugh in amazement, and at the same time we draw the girl's attention to her recent achievement. Encouraged, the mother tries to get her to say whether or not she likes milk. But now the girl is completely "out," she withdraws and does not understand anything. It is impossible to imagine her answering a question — we wonder if perhaps we just fancied the whole thing.

Almost everyone who knows these girls can describe situations similar to those related above, but the descriptions may vary. "You can never get her to follow directions, but then — when you walk away — she does what you asked for" or "she cannot cope with demands, not even her own, when she wants something and exerts herself to it, it is nearly impossible for her to manage" or "...and she suddenly realized what she was doing, and then she came to a halt in the middle of the staircase and could not take another step, despite of her bold-hearted start" or "when you make her observant somehow, if you tell her how clever she is or something, then she stops acting" or "she performs at her best if you can make her do things incidentally, so to speak."

10   Large Fluctuations in Behavior

Girls with Rett syndrome generally do have the same difficulties and exhibit great similarities in their behavior. It is still not possible to say that they are precisely so and so, or can perform this or that, since a characteristic feature of Rett syndrome is the great behavioral fluctuations. The behavior changes from day to day and even from hour to hour, and it is characterized more by extremes than by nuances. Everyone has their good and bad moments, but this is something else and different. These girls can change abruptly from tears to laughter, one mood changes into another without either them or their surroundings being able to control this process. Spells of screaming or laughter for no apparent cause, in the daytime as well as in the night, are reported for all age groups, but seem to be most common in the youngest.

These great fluctuations are a problem not only for the girls themselves but also for those around them and for the interaction between them. The girls' variations in mood and desire for contact create a feeling of powerlessness in others. Often one cannot understand their reactions and one feels that it is not possible to help them or influence the course of events. The impression a girl makes on a casual visitor depends on the time chosen for the visit. Only those in close and continuous contact with her have a chance to register all her sides, and particularly her good ones.

Every girl in my study displays these fluctuations. The basic fluctuations seem to be in degree of attention, susceptibility to impressions, and openness to the outer world. This in turn affects mood, desire, and capacity for contact and interaction with the surroundings and also the girls' performance as a whole.

One day a girl may seem grave and impossible to entice to laughter, tired and "out," just wanting to be alone. She may seem to take in neither the people nor the objects around her. If her surroundings continue to intrude, she will either overreact or not react at all to some stimuli, react with listlessness to toys she usually favors, or refuse to eat her favorite food. She can be sad or angry without any obvious cause and less susceptible to consolation. The next day, however, the picture may be all changed and she girl is alert and merry, easy to relate to, curious and interested.

She seems to "take in" better intellectually and also performs better. She appears to perceive sensory impressions more normally and can concentrate for longer periods of time — she gets on more easily with her tasks and can keep on without getting tired or forgetting what she is doing. She is impressionable in the positive sense of the word.

These are the times when a girl may suddenly astonish those around her by doing things she is "not able to" do — like grasping an object, drawing a conclusion, following directions, imitating a gesture or saying some words. It may happen only once, but those around her will notice and remember it, because her behavior is in such glaring contrast to her usual performance. "It is as if her mind is covered by clouds," says an aide, "but sometimes the clouds disperse and you can see the sky." One father compares his daughter's brain to a ball of strings and describes it like this: "...sometimes the strings are all tangled in a skein full of knots — but then, all of a sudden, all the strings are straightened out in the right direction."

[margin handwritten note: WORK... IS THERE A CORRE- LATION]

These are two very good descriptions of how these girls may appear. One gets the impression that many impulses go astray in them, that they do not reach their proper destination, and do not integrate in the correct manner, the result being misinterpretations, incorrect reactions, and sometimes no reaction at all. Sometimes the input seems to be far too large — too many impulses going in simultaneously, clashing with each other with flash-overs, short circuits and blockages as a result. The girls cannot control what happens but responds emotionally and thus a vicious circle is set up — or occasionally a favorable one.

Over the years, these strong fluctuations in attention, responsiveness, mood, performance, and overall behavior tend to slow down and be more moderate in their manifestation. The problem is still there but the girls' behavior does not change that often and to that extent. When asked about the cause of these fluctuations, most people answer that they originate within the girls, as a mere physiological phenomenon and also that they are beyond the control of other people. But, in addition, the girls are also very sensitive to different kinds of outer and inner stress; physiological as well as psychological.

Many parents stress the importance of keeping their daughters healthy. If they are in bad shape they have neither the time nor the energy for anything, other than listening to the signals of their bodies.

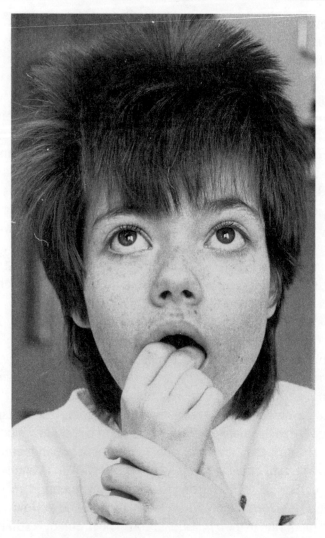

Ulrika may be really attentive and captivated by something. In the next moment she can be completely "out of it."

✱ Many people describe the girls' gastrointestinal well-being as crucial. With few exceptions, they have serious problems with constipation. If the stomach does not work nothing works. Some of them become inactive and apathetic if they have not had evacuation, while others become irritable or deeply unhappy and plagued. Once evacuation occurs a girl can be "quite a different person."

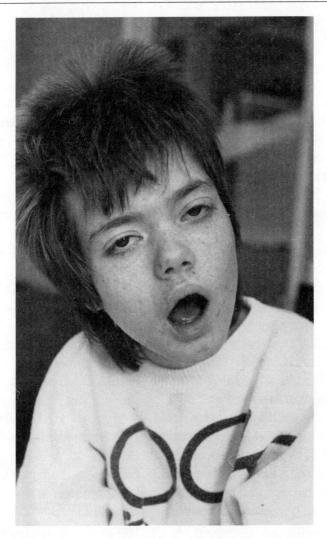

All of Ulrika droops. Her body slackens and the stereotypies cease.
Her eyes become dull and she goes into a state of isolation.

Other factors influencing the pattern of fluctuation are epilepsy,
excessive heat which has a negative influence on many of those in the
study, and infections, which many parents report hamper their daughters very badly, even if the infection itself is not a severe one.

11 Emotional Reactions

Persons with Rett syndrome have achieved certain skills and then, more or less suddenly, they lose them. Even if there have been deviations in their progress right from the beginning, as some parents claim, these deviations have mostly been concealed by the normal course of development. The little girl has been moving forwards, slowly perhaps, but still keeping her course. Her work in conquering the world has started and step by step she has begun to explore the possibilities of her body and her environment. She is capable of understanding and performing more and more, and her grip on her world is getting better and better.

Then development comes to a standstill and begins to move backwards instead. Her words do not come easily any more. She cannot control her body as before. When walking she may fall or become hesitant if the ground is ever so slightly uneven. Sometimes her body may begin to shake without her understanding why. The signals from her body may be incomprehensible or frightening or even painful. Signals which she can neither interpret nor protect herself against are rushing in on her through eyes and ears.

Those around her will notice when she stops progressing and instead loses skills already mastered. Of course the girl herself—who is living inside this strange body in this strange world — will notice as well. This incessantly gives her reasons to be surprised and disappointed, startled and frightened, unhappy and angry. Her world is no longer safe and predictable and she no longer knows her way about. She has lost her control and her foothold.

Not only has the world changed. Her own role in it has changed too. She is no longer one who knows. She is someone who does not know any more — but she cannot understand why.

I have tried to describe above a fairly typical picture of a child with Rett syndrome, but when it comes to the girls' reactions to their disorder every one has her own way of acting.

What disappointments she will experience and how she will handle her situation will vary from one girl to another. It depends on *when* her development begins to stagnate — how much she has been able to build up and how much she accordingly will lose.

If she has barely learned to sit by herself she will lose a smaller world than if she has begun to walk — but she will also have fewer disappointments. What her reactions will be depends, too, on how *fast* it all happens — whether the clash is sudden and violent, or whether the rate of progress has always been slow and she just comes to a standstill before she begins to regress equally slowly. *Who* the girl is also comes into play — whether she is a person who submits to the inevitable or protests against it, or whether she is a person who uses small or large gestures. Other problems that the girl has to cope with will also influence the picture, as, for example, infections, accidents, or alterations in the home setting. The disorder in itself can also hit the girls with varying strength, some girls getting more and also more pronounced symptoms and others fewer and milder.

[handwritten margin note: Where is Kathy?]

The child can react in various ways — and she often does. She may protest violently, screaming and crying, biting herself or fighting. She may isolate herself from the environment in a state of rest or brooding or escape. She may actively test her skills — and fail, or she may lose herself in passivity and accept her inability.

"She could place herself with her back towards all of it, and just stand there," tells one parent. "She became completely dependent on permanent routines," says another, " she had to have food at fixed times, she could only sleep in her own bed, if somebody took her little red spade she cried and fought," — "earlier she crawled between the rooms, handling things on the floor, but then she just sat there and she did not want to touch anything you offered her."

The girl needs consolation and security in her bewilderment. She must have a chance to give full expression to and be accepted in her despair and feel that love is still surrounding her. She must also experience the security of her world being restructured. She demonstrates by her behavior that she cannot cope with the world when she cannot perceive it correctly or understand what is happening. She also shows us how she herself is trying to create order in her chaotic life — by firmly clinging to what she recognizes and understands, like her own bed, a well-known toy, a particular song, fixed times, hunger and the immediate satisfaction of the stomach. It is up to us to help her gradually build confidence in more things and events in her life.

She also needs greater confidence in her own body. Even if she will never be able to win back total control of it, it is important that she does not see it as something she need be afraid of. She needs to experience joy when her body moves and that her hands should not be seen only as sources of disappointment.

When the condition gradually stabilizes and she is beginning to feel more at home in her new circumstances, life is no longer so chaotic for her. Her handicaps are still there, however, and there is always the risk of failure and frustration. The knowledge and experience of this will affect how she acts and participates in the environment. Consequently, her current behavior is not only an expression of her primary handicaps but also a result of how she has been able to handle these handicaps emotionally.

12 Insecure Identity

Girls with Rett syndrome have an incomplete and confused image of themselves. Their body awareness as well as their self-awareness is deficient. This is tied up with their handicaps, preventing them from gaining experience of the external world and of their own abilities as well. Understanding of their own abilities will also be hampered by the fact that the girls repeatedly lose the skills that they had. At one stage they lose their ability to talk and their hand motor skills. Later they may learn to walk — and then they may lose this, too. They have to rebuild their self-image over and over again. Under these circumstances it is difficult for them to know who they are and to have a positive and realistic image of themselves.

Body Awareness

These girls probably do not experience their bodies as being something controlled by themselves. The body is rather a source of uncertainty and fear; it does not respond and it plays tricks on them.

Since they have difficulty in receiving information from as well as sending information to their own bodies, their body comprehension becomes very poor. Those in the study have, on the whole, a poor body awareness, with little understanding of where the different parts of the body are placed and what they are used for. Some have learned to understand the names of some parts of the body and can benefit from this in certain situations, but the real and deep understanding is missing. This can be evidenced by the fact that some of them seem to have difficulty in understanding where the limits of their own bodies are — if, for example, one holds their hand when out for a walk, their walking sometimes seems to become more complicated because they do not seem to know who is actually in charge of it and how many legs they have to keep a check on.

Nor do they seem to be able to assess their reach or the size of their bodies in relation to their environment. They can behave as if they are uncertain if their legs will be long enough to climb over an obstacle, or they can try to grasp things far out of their reach.

Self-Awareness

Their self-awareness is uncertain, though noone within the study group is completely without some form of self-awareness. The vast majority of them know who they are in the sense that they react in some way to their name. They respond when being addressed, though there are a variety of reactions, like turning the head, smiling, ceasing the hand movements — or intensifying them. Often the girls can demonstrate that they understand that the conversation concerns them. They also know, for example, when it is their turn in the "good morning song" in school. They usually become very excited when one talks about them in a praising tone of voice. Many parents report the pride their daughters show in getting new clothes, for instance, and that in such situations they like to look at themselves in the mirror and admire their appearance. Their reaction to their reflection in the mirror on other occasions may vary from happiness and touching to confusion or withdrawal. Only a small minority show no reaction whatsoever.

KATHY RESPONDS POSITIVELY TO THE MIRROR

Self-Confidence

Confidence in their own abilities varies drastically from one girl to another, and it is not always in direct relation to their true potential. Some are more passive than necessary, not even doing what they actually are able to. Others consistently overestimate their abilities and exert themselves despite frequent failures, sometimes becoming furious when they do not meet with success. Also their conception of their ability to have an effect on their environment varies widely. At one extreme are girls who hardly ever try to convey any messages to those around them. They seem uninterested in expressing a wish or affecting the people around them. These girls take the role of passive spectators and receivers of care. The other extreme consists of those who are able to act in their environment and who may tenaciously continue trying to convey their message even in situations when it is obvious that no one but themselves understands what they want.

The reason for these varied reactions is partially attributed to individual differences in temperament, will-power, interest in the environment, and persistence. The deciding factors in their achievement in communication skills, however, is whether their attempts at communicating are noticed and received and what their previous experiences have been.

It is also noteworthy that the girls' attempts at communicating will vary depending on the circumstances. In an environment where they expect the receiver to interpret their signals they will also give many more signals for the receiver to interpret.

[handwritten margin note: MY ROLE IN COMMUNICATION]

5

GUIDELINES FOR TREATMENT AND TEACHING

1 Two Principal Teaching Groups

Some of those with Rett syndrome reach stage 4 of the illness in their early childhood years, while others are still in stage 3 in their teens. The symptoms are variable in each individual girl and as a result, it is sometimes difficult to understand that two girls of the same age who behave so differently have the same disorder. It is often impossible for a nonprofessional to judge how far the disorder has progressed, but this is not always of primary concern.

From an educational/therapeutic perspective it might prove more practical to group the girls in other ways. I have found it useful to divide them into two main groups, which to some extent correspond to the medical staging system. However, I have chosen to accentuate *HIGH* other factors. I have formed groups according to level of mobility, as there *?* seems to be a connection between tempo and mobility in these girls. *LOW* Emotional, sensory, and motor mobility seem to go together and interact.

High Degree of Mobility

Those girls who can walk or somehow move on their own (crawl, roll, walk with support) often possess an overall quicker pace. They are more active in their hand-motor effort, although they may not necessarily grasp better.

85

It is among these girls that one sees the long periods of active concentration and the sudden subsequent quick actions that come as a direct and sudden "breakthrough." Their hand stereotypies are intense as are their other stereotypies and the hyperventilation is often more pronounced in this group. They also possess an overall higher activity level and a quicker psychic (emotional and mental) tempo. They are eager and impatient and they often show more extremes than modulations in their conduct.

Complete inattention can quickly change to complete attention, and they switch from activity to passivity in an instant: "The curtain goes up and down." They give the impression of either closing out the world or being wide open and exposed to it. When they are open, strong, conflicting, and confusing impulses and impressions seem to pass through them which may lead to internal chaos. They seem to have trouble sorting out and handling the flow of incoming stimuli. There may also be difficulty in sorting and modulating the outgoing responses, both emotional and physical. It can be all or nothing; laughter or tears.

The girls in this group are active and try to deal with their environment, but they have problems in finding order in the world and in realizing the limitations of their bodies. They often fail and appear to experience many frustrations. They are in a good position because of their ability to demonstrate their needs and wants in various circumstances. To make use of their abilities, however, they require assistance to establish order in their environment. They must get to know themselves and this is difficult, since they frequently experience a lack of control — it is not they themselves who rule their bodies and emotions; rather, it is the opposite.

This group requires much help in finding order in its life. The girls need a safety zone of their own, to feel secure in order to cope with the insecure world. They may, in the true sense of the word, need their hand movements. They may also need their raggedy doll, their particular place in the corner, their picture on the wall, or whatever they have chosen as their individual security blanket in their lives. They need time, sensitivity, and respect from those of us who surround them so that they may attain a feeling of security in a wider range of situations.

In this group one finds girls who have progressed fairly well in their development before the disorder forces them to a halt. Also in this group are those in whom the illness has not yet progressed very far; which includes the majority of younger girls and a few older ones.

Lower Level of Mobility

The second group contains those girls with lesser mobility. They are often confined to a wheelchair or cannot move independently. They all have a degree of sluggishness in their movements and their pace is slower. Hand movements are less lively and the stereotypies are more subdued. The girls in this group also have delayed responses, but their periods of concentration give the appearance of deep inner thought and naturally fit their slow style. Their psychic tempo is also slower. They do not seem to be flooded by emotions and are not as prone to the same sudden impulses as the girls who demonstrate more mobility. They do not function at the extreme of the range but cluster within a smaller but more diversified part of it. Within this narrower part, they cope better than the more mobile girls. They can regulate the intensity of incoming stimuli and outgoing responses better, and their sensory integration and motor coordination is more organized. They "catch up with themselves." Their movements are better coordinated and are not shrouded by as many irrelevant movements. It is easier for those around them to "read" these girls. They usually have more distinct eye pointing, and in a way have more control over their bodies and feelings.

These girls, in a sense, are more imprisoned by their bodies than the first group, but they are more in tune with them. Within their limited area, they manage better. They exude a passive, yet more harmonious state. They live in a small world but, within it, they do not exhibit the constant conflict of wanting but being unable. This is not to say that they lack drive or energy, but that they do not persist in their drives in the same manner as the first group of girls.

Above all, those who are less mobile need continuous help in taking initiatives and performing some activities on their own. They require assistance in achieving an identity beyond that of passive spectator and receiver, the identity of a human being with confidence who braves the world. They also require a well-structured environment with sensitive people around them, who will give them the opportunity to show their real abilities. In this group are girls who were struck by the illness at an early stage of their development. There are also in this group those in whom the illness has progressed to a greater degree, which includes many of the older girls and not so many of the younger ones.

Bear in mind that "psychic tempo" is not the same as intellectual ability! However, intellectual ability may manifest itself in different ways in the two groups. It is easier to find clear evidence of accomplishment and clearly defined responses in the mobile girls. In the second group one must be more alert and may have to rely on personal intuition and sensitivity.

As I see it, there is, in the same manner, no decisive difference between the two groups when it comes to the desire to establish contact and communication with the environment, although this wish is shown in different ways and with varying intensity in the two groups. It is always hazardous to group human beings in this way. It can only be done artificially without claiming to reflect reality, which is always more complex and fluid when examined in detail. Many girls will not fit exactly into either of these groups, because they may be more multifaceted with characteristics from both groups, or because they are in the process of moving from one group to the other. However, for convenience, the above grouping may prove helpful.

2 Multihandicaps

Regardless of which group the girls belong to or at what stage of the illness they are, they are all multihandicapped and so face similar problems.

Being multihandicapped means not only that one has a variety of handicaps, adding up to a composite. These handicaps also interact in a complex relationship in which each handicap reinforces the others, so that each handicap becomes more prominent than it would have been had the person suffered from that handicap only. *[GOOD DEFINITION!]*

A severely multihandicapped child is prevented from acquiring experience to the same degree as a child with only a singular handicap. A primary learning disability, for instance, in this manner causes a secondary hindrance. The intellect is not only retarded but is also in a sense inactivated.

If one is multihandicapped one also has fewer possibilities to compensate for a handicap. One may not be able to make up for nonexisting speech by using gestures, for instance.

Being multihandicapped is also an obstacle to displaying one's actual abilities. One therefore receives poor feedback from those around, although one's need for social attention and stimulation is greater than that of other children. This situation may lead to low self-confidence, which also affects performance and hence in turn reinforces the real handicaps.

Since girls with Rett syndrome are multihandicapped, they never fully utilize their resources. To what extent they do utilize them depends largely on the environment in which they live. In each situation, they depend on us, who live with them, to enable them to make use of their resources in the best way possible.

A good educational treatment for these girls does not only include tools and practical aids. It also requires us to be and behave with the girls in such a way that progress and learning are possible. The girls need arrangements for both their physical and mental environments. A proper educational treatment goes far beyond the pure "teaching situations" and thus also has a therapeutic value. The security of the girls will grow as their understanding of the world and of their own role in it grows.

With this in mind, I have chosen not to single out individual disabilities and prescribe treatment, but rather to describe how the girls' disabilities influence their behavior within certain areas. Within these areas, I will give suggestions for practical assistance. I will also give suggestions on how to help by giving a more sensitive response.

The following is a list of the headings I will use: understanding the environment; making use of one's body; interacting and communicating with the environment; being active; expanding one's world.

3 Understanding the Environment

When the little girl's development stagnates and her life changes, she requires help in reestablishing her world before it turns into a chaos so profound that she completely loses her confidence in the world. Her life has changed and is no longer the same, she is frightened and confused and can no longer rely on her body and senses. She must rebuild her world into something she is able to comprehend and trust again. She herself gives the impression of making great efforts to create order and structure in her reality. She persists in what she knows and clings to it firmly — be it right or wrong. What she is able to sort out and recognize becomes indispensable to her. What she does not recognize or what she perceives as threatening and dangerous, she firmly discards.

Some girls adopt security symbols, objects which make their world appear safer. If these security symbols are portable, they may make the girls feel more confident in a strange environment and enable them to accept things they would otherwise have rejected.

These girls are like other small children, only more so. Since they feel less secure, their willingness to compromise is not so strong and their flexibility is more limited.

Analyzing the Individual Girl's Problems

When one wants to help, it is imperative to analyze the problems of the individual child and attempt to understand her own inherent logic or pattern of thinking. What is she afraid of and why?

If the girl, for instance, is afraid of water, did this fear originate as a result of an unpleasant experience when she took a bath, so that bathing in itself is associated with something frightening? If so, she must be given the opportunity to associate water with something enjoyable and positive, instead. She would possibly benefit from playing and having fun with water before actually taking a bath. Or does the girl find that the feel of water against her skin is an unpleasant sensation? If this is the case, maybe a bath would be more pleasant than a shower, and perhaps it would also help alleviate anxiety to increase the temperature of the water a little, so that it will not be "felt" so acutely. Does she believe that she will disappear into the water or be swallowed up by it? If so, showering or washing using cloth or sponge would be preferable to immersing her whole body in water. Is it the transition from being dry to being wet that is frightening — is she startled by the change? If this is the case, one should let her approach the water gradually, to get acquainted with the feeling of being wet before her entire body is submerged.

It is not a question of spoiling or being overprotective, but rather of showing consideration. The child's world must be conceivable to her before she dares to participate in it. In order to make this possible one must choose carefully among the situations the girl is exposed to — some are unavoidable or more necessary than others. In addition, she needs help in understanding what is taking place within those chosen situations. Actually the parents do not have much of a choice. The girl's distress is often so intense that she, herself, provokes the solutions she needs. As a result, one automatically limits stimuli to those most necessary, and endeavors to make them clear and positive.

The Girls Require Concrete and Positive Experiences

The little girl needs to have her world re-explained. Her experiences must be basic and simplified, so that she is better able to understand the given situation. If she is to understand her experiences they must also, in some way, be about and affect herself.

That which is meaningful to her, that which carries a positive association, for example, is easier for her to understand, to learn, and to remember. Thus, the sound created during the preparation of food is much more likely to be interpreted and remembered than a sound created by an activity which has no significance for the girl.

If a situation can be created so that attention is maximized and directed solely towards one object, the girl's senses are given the opportunity to cooperate and take in the entire message. In this manner, the senses can support each other and work together, rather than compete for attention and disrupt each other.

Presenting and Structuring Time

Routines and Rituals. It will be easier for the girls to understand the meaning of what is happening to them, if the signals from the environment can be arranged so that certain key signals always appear together and in a fixed sequence. Consequently, routines and rituals will constitute an important framework in their lives.

The disadvantage with routines is that, using them as props, the girl may become dependent upon them. The ritual becomes meaningful for her and she has difficulty breaking away from it, whether the routine has been created for a purpose or quite by chance. For example, the little girl who cried in the hallway knew that usually one goes to the store, first, and, afterwards, one goes home. It was not devastating for her when there was a change from the routine, since she already perceived her world as safe and secure. Nevertheless, she was disturbed at the upset in her schedule, and it was fortunate that her mother understood why her daughter was unhappy and could respect and handle her reactions.

Schedule. To create routines is to structure time. Time is divided into identifiable portions, and through her own concrete experiences the girl develops understanding and meaning in reference to concepts such as "now" and "later," "before" and "after," "today" and "tomorrow." Routines offer the girl an opportunity to understand exactly what is happening at a given time, and to prepare herself for what is about to occur.

Knowing the names of the days is of no significance whatsoever, unless each day is associated with something specific. For example, what is so special about a Wednesday? One must assign a distinctive significance to that day, so that it stands out from the other days. Perhaps, Wednesday could be the day when one drives to the public pool for a swim. What is, then, special about a Friday? Well, for many, Friday is the last school day in the week. It is of no small importance to the child to know this, so that she does not expect to attend school on Saturday morning, and becomes confused and perhaps unhappy, when the school bus does not come. Since one is not sure of the completeness of these girls' verbal understanding, one must also give continual support in the form of concrete experiences. In many schools there are special "Friday routines," which can be used on other days as well, for instance, before holidays. Perhaps there is a morning circle which is different in form and content from that of the other days, or a special Friday activity or "Friday song" at the end of the day. Often the child needs further signals at home as well. Putting her school bag in a special weekend "parking spot" is a clear signal which can be used to explain longer holidays as well. As long as her school bag is placed in the wardrobe, for instance, school is out. On Saturday morning, a breakfast served in a different manner, with lighted candles or on a particular tablecloth, will reinforce her understanding that there is no school today. One girl in the sample wears pants to school and a skirt at weekends, and this distinction probably serves as a significant signal to her. On Sunday evening, it may be enough to take the girl's school bag out from the "parking spot" and place it by her bed. When she wakes up and sees her bag, she knows it is time for school again, and she receives further reinforcement when the bag is packed.

The need for being prepared also means that scheduling is of primary importance. All days should have a recurring basic rhythm, which is consistently repeated from day to day, and those activities which differentiate the days from one another should always fall on the same day of the week. To enable the girl to "read" her particular schedule, it must be presented to her in a concrete way. Simply telling her that "today is Wednesday and you are going to swim" may not be enough. Seeing her swimsuit being packed into her bag makes it more likely that she will understand the meaning of the words. If she is not going to the pool directly in the morning, she will need further preparation during the day. During morning circle in school, one may also talk about today being swimming day, show a picture of the swimming pool, and fetch the children's bags, showing that they have all brought their swimsuits. In this way one prepares ahead and makes the connection in the girl's memory of her parents packing her swimsuit in the morning. Perhaps the class has the swim session after lunch. Prior to the lesson the children are gathered again and prepared for the experience, by talking about swimming and by seeing and touching their swimsuits. Then, when the girl is being dressed in her outdoor clothes, she knows why. She is not going home, or out for a walk. She is not going to the store. She is going to the swimming pool. Nobody puts on their outdoor clothes without a reason, but if the girl does not know the reason she will probably make a guess, with a risk of guessing wrong and feeling let down. She may become angry or unhappy, without her caregiver understanding why.

In this way, clear signals are created and time is structured day by day, hour by hour. Each day has its own special content, and each hour of the day has its own meaning and place in the schedule: now we eat and afterwards we go outside. First the apron goes on, then to the cooking lesson. After the assembly there will be gymnastics.

Understanding When a Situation Begins and Ends. When the girl is insecure and confused, rituals and routines may become vital. If the food, for instance, does not arrive at the proper time and when she is expecting it, her reaction is often so great that she cannot eat the food at all when it does come. She simply cries. To abandon fixed eating times in a situation like this, in order to help the child to get rid of her fixed ideas is no solution, but will only increase her confusion and sense of being left out. She may, however, need help in acquiring more realistic expectations — something that helps her to understand *when* the food is actually supposed to arrive.

Mealtimes are often difficult situations. It is important that they function well, since they occur frequently and affect the well-being of the entire family. However, mealtimes can be frustrating for the girl. We cannot be sure that hunger is always the triggering factor when she expects food. Perhaps she is very fond of food and has learned that setting the table is a sign that food is coming. Thus, when she hears or sees the table being set, she prepares herself in her stomach and heart for food. On the other hand, she does not have a proper appreciation of time. Some time elapses between the table being set and the actual meal being served, and this time often varies from one meal to another. Sometimes the girl may become very impatient. "Soon," one might say. "Wait a while." She may have some understanding of the word "wait." It means "not now." But after a while it is not "now" anymore and she has waited. "Soon" is a completely incomprehensible word, which can mean anything from seconds to hours, and most likely she has not learned such a useless word.

At last the food is ready and served. The girl sits at the table with her bib on and waits. An adult prepares her food, and tastes it to check the temperature. Surely it is the child, herself, who is finicky about the food not being too hot, but it is by no means certain that she comprehends the word "hot." "Hot" could very well mean "not now" from her experience. There is no guarantee that she pays any attention whatsoever to what the adult says; his words could be sounds among other sounds. *She*, for her part, concentrates on her plate and on the food placed on it. She looks carefully at it. When nothing happens she tries to signal in other ways; and if she has to wait for a long time, she may start screaming. In her eyes, the adult's behavior is inconsistent. Sometimes one eats immediately, other times one does not. From the girl's point of view, everything is ready. The china, food, family, and herself are all where they should be. The bib is on, the food is on her plate, the adult has even *eaten* some of it. She is ready and she is communicating this fact in any way she can.

This is just an example, but it represents a type of situation in which the girl is liable to find herself time after time. She understands, yet she does not. She has learned that she has a role in a given situation, but she does not really know when her role begins. If one could give her a signal, a sign which told her that "*now*, neither sooner or later, is the time to prepare for the actual eating, because right away the first spoonful of food will arrive" this would help her during her waiting, and the meal would be more peaceful for everybody. What signal should be chosen depends on who the girl is and to what family she belongs. One method could be to use her bib in a more systematic manner.

The girl's bib is something that is close to her, perceived by several senses, and easily understood. Moreover, using the bib as a signal does not impede the other eaters. If one waits to put the bib on until the "right" moment, preferably with some ritual which makes the girl pay attention to what is happening, she receives the sign she needs and will gradually be able to handle the situation better.

To demonstrate that an activity is over is just as important as to mark its commencement. To understand whether a meal is over or not is not very easy. Sometimes there is a dessert, sometimes not — sometimes it arrives directly, and sometimes one has to wait again. "Off with the bib!" is a clear signal that the girl will understand, if it comes off consistently when there is no more food to be expected.

If the girl is given a clear association, as described above, she will hopefully little by little learn to stretch her patience up to the bib. If not, she might easily perceive mealtime either as a situation over which she has no control, which leads to resignation, or as a situation in which she really has to kick up a fuss to get food.

A sign that is transferable from place to place, like a bib, is advantageous because it can be used at a friend's home, or when travelling. It would be a bad idea to teach the girl an association which cannot be consistently adhered to because it is too artificial or cumbersome. She has enough disappointments already, due to those incorrect associations she herself makes. Therefore, it is better to use "natural ingredients" but in a systematic manner. The bib, of course, is just an example. Other appropriate signals could be to push the child's chair to and from the table at the proper moment, or consistent joining hands to say grace, a little game, or a rhyme.

In the same way as the girl is prepared for "now it is about to begin," she must be given an opportunity to prepare for "now it is about to end." Clear signals could be, in this example, to say "now comes the last spoonful," and then to take her hands and perform the sign for "finished" and take off the bib after the last bite of food has been swallowed.

It is also important to really bring a situation to its close, and not to interrupt it untimely without a reason. Such a situation becomes inconsistent and the girl will have difficulty in understanding both the situation and her own part in it.

Signals. One can choose words, signs, pictures, tangible symbols, activities, and various combinations of these to explain different situations. Combining several signals is beneficial, because the situation is clarified when several senses support one another, and because appealing to more than one channel makes it easier to reach the girl if she has poor concentration.

Music. Singing as an educational tool is very beneficial to the child. In many schools there are different kinds of "good morning songs" and "good-bye songs." There are songs that tell the children "now we are to eat food," — "now it is time to go brush our teeth," — "now it is time to go to the gymnasium," — "after this song it is time to leave the swimming pool."

Girls with Rett syndrome are often very fond of and captivated by music, though there are exceptions. They are fascinated by voices. They enjoy adults playing with their voices and whispering to them instead of speaking. Many parents point out that their daughters "understand better" when words are sung to them, rather than merely spoken. Girls with Rett syndrome perceive rhythm strongly and are somehow engrossed by it. Their hand movements often demonstrate a rigidly rhythmic make-up; and when they stamp their feet, rock and breathe, they do it to their own special beat. It is then only natural to make use of this passion and to use it as much as possible when dealing with the girls socially as well using it therapeutically and to facilitate learning.

Singing during an activity is also a good idea. If one is consistent both in the choice of songs and in their relative position, singing can give substance to concepts such as "now" and "later." To most people music leads to an intense creation of associations. When one hears the first few notes of a tune, one not only knows what song is being played, one also is reminded of a whole situation which in some way is associated with that particular tune, and the circumstances and events of that situation are recalled together with the emotions and feelings originally felt in the situation. Music also creates associations in other ways. It makes us "remember forward." For instance, when listening to a familiar record, one often knows at the end of a song which song will follow. Even if one hears a piece of music for the first time, one knows when it is over, as opposed to its being interrupted before the end.

In schools, it is rather common to use music in order to help the girls to understand and anticipate various activities. Music is frequently used with gymnastics and physical therapy, for example. Ready-made music programs are used when putting the joints through their full range of motion. For other kinds of mobility training, the therapist sometimes makes up her own songs and so do parents and assistants. Ready-made programs or not, the main thing is consistency. The different exercises/movements should always appear in the same order, and the same song should be used for the same movement. Without such consistency music helps to make physical training enjoyable and fun. With consistency it helps the girls to understand as well. They learn which exercise and which movement comes next and get a chance to cooperate. They will learn how long a particular exercise will last and anticipate the end of laborious, tiresome exercise routines. Music also helps the adult to perform the exercises properly, gently, and rhythmically, and for a suitable length of time.

Presenting and Structuring Space

As with time, space must be presented to and structured for the girl. She lives in both.

It is important for her to have the opportunity to explore a new room by moving through it bodily, looking at it from various angles and perspectives. If she is unable to move about herself for the purpose of exploring in this way, she must be helped to do so, on foot, or in a wheelchair, or in somebody's arms. She must be allowed to find herself high and low and examine the room from different positions. She must be allowed to experience not only the room but also its limits and its relationship to other rooms. In order to understand the room, she must experience it in relation to her own body and with all her senses. The more immobile she is, the more assistance she requires from others to do this.

"Space" is also space and time in relation to one another. One learns what is near and what is far away by experiencing how long and how many steps it takes to move a certain distance.

The physically disabled person must also rely on the eyes for measurement. The girl could increase her understanding of the room by visually tracking a ball rolling across the floor or a light being moved around the ceiling and walls. This technique also trains the eye's ability to accommodate, and expands the child's spatial sphere of interest.

The girl must not only understand what a room is. In order for her to find her way, she must appreciate the room's position in relation to other rooms. She must be able to identify the various rooms. In unfamiliar surroundings, she may select some detail (a painting, a special chair, a rug, a radiator) which later helps her to recognize the room. This is a good method, but is not always reliable. The girl's associations are governed by the preferences of her senses, if she has nothing else to fall back on, and such associations are often random and incorrect. For instance, she may pick out something that catches her attention without it being relevant in the given situation. Associating a room with a car standing outside the window with blinkers on the roof will not help her to recognize the room the next time she is there and the car is gone.

Better associations can be formed if the room also has a more functional meaning for her. Those rooms that are familiar to her are often identified according to their function (toilet = tinkle, hallway = go outside). These types of associations build a better foundation for generalization. A girl who associates a kitchen with eating food will have similar expectations of food in all kitchens. The combination of the kitchen's characteristic details (stove, sink) and the knowledge of the function of the kitchen make this room very important to the girls, who are usually very fond of food. The appearance of the kitchen is consequently something that is easy for them to identify and register correctly in the memory. Many people tell how girls in a new environment are immediately able to find the kitchen and remember its location at their next visit.

The ability to recognize gives security and creates anticipations. A conscious attempt to give context to each room, where the girl often stays, through demonstrating the room's function, facilitates her effort to create a spatial structure. It might be beneficial, therefore, to tie certain activities to individual rooms. Likewise, in an environment that is new to the girl but where she will frequently be in the future, (for example, the bathroom), it would be easier for the girl to not change her diapers anywhere except in the bathroom, or, in the case of physiotherapy, not to conduct it here and there, but instead select a special room or place for that activity. In this way, the girl will understand the rooms and their functions more quickly and when being moved will be prepared for changes of activity. In this way, she will also be better able to show what she herself wants and means.

Presenting Objects

In the same way, objects are made discernible and comprehensible to the girl. They should be made perceptually clear, and the girl must be allowed to explore their characteristics and functions.

Through their own experiences children gain understanding of concepts such as quality and quantity. Different objects feel different in the hand, and they smell and taste and sound different; they function in different ways; and there may be one or more of the same object. Children who are able to move around the room and to grasp objects explore them in this way. They manipulate, drop, and throw the objects, and so learn many things about objects and space, about cause and effect, and about their own part in the situation. Different objects sound different when they fall on the ground, for instance. The sound also depends on where they land — on the carpet or on the wooden floor, on the grass or on the gravel. These girls may not be able to create such experimental situations themselves, and, they probably have not finished their early exploration of their environment, when the disorder prevented them from going on. Thus, one may now have to create those situations for them, offering them different items of many types of modalities and in many different situations.

By experience the girl will also learn the purpose of different objects. One uses a spoon to eat food, a tooth brush to brush teeth. The degree of her understanding of objects will also affect her performance. If she knows what a tape recorder is all about, she will act in a different way than if she just sees an uninteresting black box.

Presenting People

The people in the girl's environment will establish their importance to her through the actions they perform together with her. Before becoming familiar with a person in this way, she will identify that person by using the same principles as when identifying any object — according to appearance and behavior. Here again, there is a risk of focusing on something inappropriate. If she were to focus on a pretty necklace or a red dress, this would not enable her to recognize (or accept) that person the next time, when she is not wearing the necklace or if dressed in black pants instead of the beautiful dress. However, from their reactions we can conclude that the girls do identify and generalize from inadequate details. One little girl, for instance, had become very fond of a neighbor who one day had joined the family for a meal. The following day she returned to visit the child, with whom she had made such excellent contact, but this time she was completely ignored. Not until the neighbor took off her jacket and showed her pretty blue blouse again did the girl react, and after that their fine contact was reestablished. Another child is very fond of her grandfather, who always wears a peaked cap. All men wearing peaked caps are met with laughing anticipation by that girl. Still another, who had been frightened in physiotherapy, was for a long time afterwards wary of women with red hair. Her parents were convinced that their daughter mistook these women for the therapist, who had red hair.

Sometimes the girls arrange their environment in such a way that they have difficulty in accepting things and persons they know and understand if these things and persons are taken out of familiar context. An example would be the girls' reactions when their parents visit their school, or a teacher comes to their home. They are not met with at all the same recognition and joy they would have received had they been in their "right" place.

If the girl is given ample time and repeated opportunities to get acquainted with a person, her associations will become more complex and correct. In the beginning of the relationship, however, there may sometimes be a reason for using the girl's own methods. If it is important for her to identify a person who seldom comes to the house, this person could make herself distinguishable by always wearing clothes of the same color or with some interesting detail. Also, if a person is called by several different names, it may be practical to teach the girl just one name at a time. At any rate, you should not mention the person, when talking about him, by any name that you are not sure that the girl can distinguish and associate correctly.

A Consistent Structure Provides Security to the Girl and Her Environment

In time, the girl's world will become more orderly. She will learn the purpose of objects, the meaning of sounds, what belongs to what. She learns when, how, and where, and also what is expected of her. Step by step, she will regain the feeling of participation and control. The more she understands, the less vulnerable she is. When she is secure in her world, her world will no longer come apart if, for instance, the picture no longer hangs in its usual place above her bed. Still, the environment may seem more comfortable if the picture continues to hang there in its place. A quick look to make sure that everything is in its proper place is an evening ritual for many girls.

When the girl's life is structured, her inner security improves. She is "with us" instead of being contrary or an outsider. Without having to constantly struggle to structure and create order among all the stimuli in her life, or having to defend herself against them, she will have more time to behave in a constructive manner. As her confidence increases, we can offer her more experiences, and experiences that are less structured and more complex.

The more the girl is helped to rebuild her reality, the more benefit she receives. She should be given time and repetition. By creating situations in which she can concentrate her attention on certain details, and by forming associations among these details, we can show her what is relevant and how it should be interpreted.

In order to make the environment understandable to the girl, details that are considered important and proper should be made very distinguishable to her. These details should be made very simple and attractive, perceptually as well as functionally. The girl's actions or expressive behavior often give hints as to how to go about creating experiences for her — whether we should use a special color or form, whether to use light, sound, or movement to capture her interest.

Participating in and structuring the girl's world in this way, is practical and secure for everyone involved. Primarily, the structure will be more reliable and "correct" this way. Secondly, those around her will have a better chance of understanding her and how she views the world. The more we understand her, the more of this knowledge we can transmit to other people around her and, in that way, we increase her security and well-being.

4 Using the Body

The girls need to acquire a better understanding of their bodies, in much the same way as they need to attain a better understanding of their environment.

These girls lack the ability to perform certain movements, or to perform them correctly, due to apraxia, ataxia, low muscle tone, and later rigidity and spasticity. They also have problems interpreting the signals they receive from their own bodies. They misinterpret or overestimate these signals, and often react fearfully. They are in danger of becoming more inactive than necessary, and a vicious circle begins.

Physical training must therefore seek to increase body awareness, as well as motor ability and motor control.

Body Concept. The girl with Rett syndrome needs continuous encouragement to engage in physical activity in order to develop better body awareness. She needs to regain the confidence in and familiarity with her body as much as possible. Even if her body will not perform as she intends it to, she can learn how her body reacts, and what the results of her movements are.

Her understanding of her body is increased by daily activities, when playing, bathing, dressing, or in gymnastics and physiotherapy, when the adult touches, moves, and at the same time uses the names of the different parts of the body. Both systematic stroking and massage of the face and body will also increase body awareness and promote mental and physical relaxation, while at the same time offering the opportunity for contact and cooperation.

Physiotherapy. Physiotherapy will always play an important part in these girls' lives. Whether the physiotherapist serves as the monitor or as an instructor for other adults, she is the person responsible for the exercise program, training the girls' movements and balance. The grls may need to practice crawling, walking, pulling themselves to a standing position, rising from and sitting down on a chair, and walking on various types of surfaces. Many of them may also need to have their joints regularly put through their full range of motion to prevent muscle wastage and decreased mobility; and one usually has to work hard to encourage the girls to use their arms for weight bearing and protective responses. The girls need a variety of equipment — standing frames, walkers, wheelchairs, tilt-boards, special chairs, lifts, therapy balls and rolls, wedges, and helmets. Some need scoliosis jackets or leg braces. The physiotherapist is also usually the person who suggests special activities such as swimming and riding.

Gross Motor Skills

These girls have the same need as other children of gross motor stimulation, but the need for extensive and varied movements cannot always be satisfied through their own activities. They require assistance in performing the movements, as well as in experiencing the movements as something positive and enjoyable.

This is the first, and perhaps the primary, task of the physical therapist — and also her greatest challenge. In as much as these girls will require physical therapy throughout their entire lives, it is important that the experience from the beginning be as positive as possible.

Generally, the initial contact between the patient and the physiotherapist takes place during the most distressing phase of the disorder. The girl is having a hard time, discriminating between the signals from the outer world, and at the same time she feels uncertain about the signals from her own body. She may be afraid of strangers. When a stranger then comes and starts handling her body, she may become even more frightened and confused. The physiotherapist may have to spend a long time in getting to know the girl, establishing a good relationship with her, before the real treatment can begin. In some cases the physiotherapist may have to demonstrate the exercises on her doll only, and in the beginning leave the actual execution of the movements to the parents. If one starts gently, and gradually introduces new exercises, the girl will have time to grow accustomed to them and to understand what is happening. If right from the start a decision is made on a specific order for the different parts of the training program, and this order is adhered to, the girl will have an even better chance to understand the situation and to accept the help she needs. As mentioned previously, a still better idea would be to also associate a special song with each part of the program.

If the girls are given gross motor experiences in situations where they feel secure, they will get increased opportunities to perceive their bodies as sources of joy and pleasure. This in turn is of great importance for their development in general. Many people describe how, after this kind of training, these girls start appreciating movements they previously feared, and how they will laugh with anticipation in a situation where they previously were pale and shaky with fright.

Riding. About a quarter of the those in the study take horseback riding for training balance. For several of them, riding is a new activity, which means that not much can be said of it, as yet. In those cases, however, where a sufficient period for introduction was allowed, and the girls have had time to get accustomed to the environment, the horse, and all aspects of the activity, the results have been very positive. Their poor initial balance has been replaced by a considerably better balance on horseback, and in addition they have found the activity very satisfying. The stereotypic hand movements have diminished, since the hands have been given something purposeful and necessary to do, as the girls have to use them in order not to lose their balance. (Each of them has an assistant to give physical help in staying in the saddle, but they also have a built up handle to hold on to.) The contact with the horse, and the feeling of "being able to" have been gratifying to the girls.

Certainly more of these girls would benefit from riding, but it is important to realize that considerable time is needed, in order to allow the riding to start with a minimum of stress, and then to continue for a sufficiently long time, as it takes time for the girls to find their rhythm and balance and to relax physically and mentally.

Activities on Their Own. One effect of Rett syndrome is that mobility and motor activity deteriorate with advancing age. Even those girls who do walk and continue walking independently will do so more stiffly as the years pass. They become more sluggish in their movements, and they will have greater difficulties in getting started. When they have the opportunity to keep on moving for a while, they become more supple and steady in their movements. On the other hand, they tire easily. Scoliosis and spasticity are symptoms which appear later in the disorder, and the girls require more and more assistance in order to maintain their mobility. It becomes important to help the girls to move from one position to another, and they need special treatment to prevent contractions of the joints.

There is, however, a difference between moving your own body and having someone else do it for you. Independently-generated activities create a different kind of experience, physically as well as emotionally. Girls characterized by gross motor passivity require encouragement to move their bodies on their own, and need to experience that they themselves can perform movements that are stimulating or lead to something enjoyable and meaningful. Trampolines, "ball baths," waterbeds, or similar things to lie on, are examples of devices used in schools for this purpose.

<u>Swimming</u>. In water even the passive girls become more active. Three-quarters of those in the study have access to warm pool baths, with regular motion exercises. On the whole, swimming is well liked, provided that the water is sufficiently warm (some girls require temperatures in excess of 90° F or 32.2° C). In the pool the girls relax, and they can

move more freely and experience better body control. Several are able to move about on their own in the pool, helped by flotation devices.

With increasing age and deteriorating mobility, some girls in the study change their behavior. Problems associated with leaving the water begin to occur. Those who still are able to walk refuse to do so. Those who need to be lifted strain their muscles and cry. There is no known reason for this behavior. Perhaps the change of temperature is troublesome, or perhaps those girls are not sufficiently prepared for the ending of the session, or maybe they are disappointed at having to leave something enjoyable. Then again, the explanation could be the contrast between feeling light and mobile in the water, against feeling heavy and restricted out of it. Whatever the reason, one must take pains to ease the transition, in order to make the entire swimming situation a positive experience. Prepare carefully, play and entice, wrap them in warm towels and friendly hands, give them all the attention and physical help necessary. This is not the situation that calls for training in walking up stairs or other exercises.

By and large, warm pool baths are so enjoyable and beneficial to the girls that they all should have the opportunity of regular swim sessions, at least once a week.

Gross Motor Activity — Sensory Training. Gross motor activity can also serve as sensory training. For one thing, movements involving the entire body are in themselves very informative. For another, the movements affect the vestibular system, which in turn affects other sensory systems of the brain. In this way, gross motor stimulation makes it easier for the girls to receive and respond to various types of signals.

For example, the girl in my own class is noticeably more "talkative" after she has been swinging in a blanket, and she is able to "loosen up" mentally when her arms are "loosened" from her body and engaged in large movements. Several people report that the girls "open up mentally," and that their understanding is improved after strong motor stimulation. I have previously described how I checked the picture comprehension of a little girl, who performed very well. Before the test, she and her caregiver had enjoyed a session of gross motor activity, which surely contributed to her remarkable concentration — we were able to keep working for a good half hour.

Ulrika loves the water. She is excited and happy, and the contact with her is excellent.

Katarina helps her to jump up and down in the water.

This exercise does not frighten Ulrika or cause her to "lose her balance."

This is just fun!

Hand Motor Skills

After the first crisis associated with the onset of the syndrome, the girls once again turn their attention to the world around them. Now, they can no longer do what they want with their hands, but this does not mean that they have lost the desire to try. Some are persistent in their efforts, while others give up relatively soon. Some adopt a negative attitude towards their hands and refuse to let others help them with tasks they can no longer perform by themselves.

In the beginning, the girls often display signs of experiencing the conflict between a desire to do something and their inability to perform. This conflict seems to have a frustrating impact on them and, in many ways, is difficult to handle for all concerned. If a girl, for example, tries to grab a cake on the table, and instead happens to pull off the tablecloth, tip over the cups, or send the dishes crashing to the floor, this is not the result she wanted. She has, however, despite her failure, clearly demonstrated her desire and will.

If the situation described above is repeated often, it is possible, of course, that the result of the mishap — the dishes crashing to the floor, the resulting noise, all the activity from the people around her, voices and movements — will become an end in itself, if this is the best the girl can do, and if she does not get so many other chances to use her hands. Still, she has demonstrated that she has will and desire. Moreover, she has shown that she needs something to do, and that she needs activities that will make it possible for her to affect her environment. This is a good starting point!

The challenge is how to respond to the girl's needs, and at the same time find activities suitable for those uncooperative hands. In almost all situations there are more ways of acting incorrectly than correctly. Other people learn the proper way to do things, but for the girls with Rett syndrome it is always easier to get it wrong. Performing incorrectly causes many problems. The girls become disappointed, and they meet negative reactions from their environment which mainly focus on — or has to focus on — the consequences of their attempts, rather than on the intentions behind them. Frequent and repeated failures may lead the girls into an increasingly passive life, where they finally stop trying.

To a large extent, the self-image of these girls is determined by the relationship between "right" and "wrong." To help them restore their self-confidence, it is essential to find out what they still *can* do and help them experience as many "rights" as possible. The people around them have to understand that "right" is what leads to the intended result, not the manner in which the task is performed. The girls cannot be taught advanced motor skills because of their major handicaps, but one can compensate for those handicaps by providing various kinds of assistance. This may be simply moving a girl's hand/arm to perform an activity or creating a situation which is better adapted to her particular abilities. The girls may also be aided by various types of technical devices.

Physical Assistance. The stereotypic hand movements usually prevent all other hand functions, and sometimes the girls cannot manage to separate their wringing hands without assistance from others. Sometimes it is helpful to hold one hand in order to make the other "available" for activities. For the girl to understand and learn a specific movement, physical guidance may be needed in the beginning, the adult holding and directing her hand with his own.

One must attempt to interpret the girl correctly, so as not to intervene too early. If she is still occupied in sizing up a situation as a preparation for action, or if she is content with looking only, an attempt from the adult to direct her body will prove a disturbance rather than being helpful. The girl must have the desire as well as "scope to spare" to accept this form of help correctly.

When, in the most disturbed phase of the disorder, the girls react as if their hands have changed into something artificial and frightening, one should be wary of using force to help them to grasp something when they refuse to use their hands. During this stage of the disorder, fine motor skills should not be given primary attention. On the contrary, these children should be shown that the hands are not dangerous, but can give positive experiences, through activities such as splashing in water or sensing the rhythm or beat in songs and rhymes. Generally, the desire to use the hands for grasping will gradually return.

When the demand for action originates within themselves, it is easier for the girls to accept help to accomplish what they themselves cannot do, but even when they demonstrate a desire to grasp an object, for instance, one must be sensitive to their reactions. The girl may still become confused or frightened when someone else moves her limbs or touches her in a wrong way. She may be afraid of losing her balance, or she may have difficulty in sorting the incoming sensory impulses induced by the actions of the helper. She may also have problems "catching up" if the pace of the adult is different from her own.

Various stimuli in the environment may adversely affect the girls, so that they suddenly are not "present" any more. Keeping their desire for the activity alive, by removing disturbances and distracting stimuli, is at least as important as helping their hands to move. Furthermore, if their own desire is clearly directed towards the goal, the unavoidable disturbance caused by the help of the adult will not be noticed as much as when the request for acting originates externally.

Adapting the Circumstances - Physical Environment. One can also respond to the girls' needs by better adaptation of their environment to their disabilities. This may involve providing them with easy-to-grasp items or objects that react correctly even though the girls cannot grasp in the real sense of the word. They grasp with the palm of their hands and do not usually use their fingers only. Thus, it is difficult for them to pick up small objects (but if their hands are very sticky and wet with saliva, the objects often get stuck to them simply because of that — and this is something the girls sometimes use to their advantage). My own student, for instance, could not pick up a flat cookie from the table, but could manage an Italian bread stick better. The bread stick was easier to grasp, and it was easier for her to take a bite from it, since it was long enough not to disappear inside her hand.

For many, water serves as an activating or relaxing element, making it easier for them to grasp an object lying in a pan of water than to grasp objects from a table, for instance. If a girl, due to poor coordination, is likely to knock an object out of her reach, although her intention was to grasp it, one can create a situation in which she will not be so frustrated. A table or a wheelchair tray with raised edges prevents objects from rolling on to the floor and increases her opportunities to repeat the movement often enough, to eventually enable her to succeed in grasping the object.

Technical Help. The girl who wants to hold on to an object, but cannot maintain her grip, may become very frustrated and give up the entire enterprise. One way to help her is to fix the object to her hand. Spoons with loops or cuffs or special mugs are examples of such solutions. However, only a few of those in this study use such devices. To make the movement necessary to get the food into the mouth, while at the same time manipulating the implements, seems to be too complicated for many of them. Since their hands, because of their stereotypic movements, clench and unclench all the time, the girls receive repeated tactile information from the utensil in the hand, and this continuous information probably acts as a disturbance in such a situation.

Though only a couple of them successfully manage utensils at mealtime, a greater number utilize implements in musical situations. Here also, they require devices to keep the implements in their hands, and they accept these much more readily than those used when eating. A drumstick might, for instance, be built up with a sponge cuff or attached to the hand with a piece of velcro. However, most of the girls do not have the coordination skills necessary for using implements. Still, of course, they may want to make music. Perhaps they could get results by directly touching the musical instruments. Perhaps they need some other kind of help, for instance, bells attached to mittens or bracelets (or, of course, to headbands or socks/slippers). The bells provide a pleasant sound when touched or simply stirred by the girls' movements.

The most common types of technical aids are various switches, which are attached to battery-operated toys or appliances such as lights, tape recorders, slide projectors, or foot spas. Depending on the girl's different abilities, the switches can be activated by pressure plates, levers, touch buttons, or photo cells. Usually the switches have to be designed in accordance with the needs of the individual girl. This is probably the reason why only nine of those in the sample use switches at all. Three of them have switches designed specifically for them.

The Purpose of Motion

When the girls are encouraged to use their hands, we must ask ourselves why, and if it is of any value to them. Hands are useful for much more than grasping — and when we grasp, we do so not only for the sake of grasping. There is an additional purpose beyond that.

Exploring the Environment. When small children take hold of and handle various objects, they at the same time acquire information about the world around them. Different objects act differently. They vary in weight. They sound different when falling to the floor. Some roll, others do not.

Often, we handle objects in order to estimate shape, weight, and quality. Girls with Rett syndrome do not have the same opportunity to gain information about objects in this manner, even if we put items into their hands. The information obtained by just holding an object in one's hand is not as satisfying as manipulating it is, and the effort needed not to drop the object does not leave much scope for anything else. If the girls are induced to vary their grip, for instance, if we place sound-making objects in their hands (like rustling paper or whistle toys), they will gain more information. (Likewise, if the girls have stereotypies repeatedly clenching and unclenching their hands, without completely opening them, they will automatically get more information from the objects in their hands.)

To fix objects in the hands, by velcro or masking tape, for instance, is a good idea. For many girls it might be more beneficial, however, to surround their hands with objects, rather than to place objects in their hands. If the girls have the opportunity to place their hands in a pan filled with sand, snow, leaves, flour, beads, beans, chains, balls — anything you like, singly or in different combinations — they will have a better chance of exploring the material and understanding the information. They can sense the quality of the objects; they themselves can make sounds and movements; and they themselves can decide whether to be active or passive. In this situation, too, the stereotypic hand movements contribute to the girls gaining more knowledge about their environment. The movements of the arms and the plucking of the hands continuously change the stimuli, and provide the girls with an opportunity to learn gradually how to make the most of certain movements. The advantage of placing the hands in things as against placing things in the hands is also that the objects in a pan, for instance, do not disappear in the same vexing way, as an object placed in the hand so often does, when it is dropped or enclosed by the hand.

Increasing the Sensitivity of the Hands. Massaging the palms with a brush or a vibrator increases the sensitivity of the hands and also makes them more ready to respond to various kinds of tactile stimulation. One can use objects of different temperatures and textures to further increase the tactile sensitivity of the hands. Sandpaper and velvet give entirely different sensations. There is a vast difference between holding a brush and holding a cake of soap. A container of warm fingerpaints offers an entirely different sensation from that of a bucket of cold snow. An ice cube in a pail of warm water provides contrasting sensations. In this way, the girls will also continuously receive information about the qualities of the surroundings.

Increasing Muscle Strength. One can give the girls objects of gradually increasing weight in order to increase their muscle strength. Tempting items can also be attached to a firm support in such a way (with velcro or magnets, for instance) that some exertion is necessary to pry them loose.

Promoting a Firmer Grip. An object that feels so pleasant to the hand that the girl really wants to hold on to it could be used to promote a firmer grip. The object should also have the quality of giving stronger and more gratifying sensations the harder the hand grasps it. A small electric vibrator or a piece of waxed paper are examples of such objects.

Promoting Arm Movements. Placing tempting objects at a progressively increasing distance will motivate the girls to extend their arms. If a specific movement is desired (like raising the arms, holding the hand still, pulling the arm towards the body) one can, for instance, design switches that require and encourage such movements.

Automatic Movements. Despite the limitations of automatic movements, acquiring such movements might still be of some value to these girls. They will reach a higher level of cooperation or independence in certain situations, which makes things easier for all concerned and improves the girls' self-esteem. Often these movements are learned spontaneously, by repeating an activity in the same way a sufficient number of times, as in everyday situations. One can, of course, arrange situations where the girls are induced or helped to perform something so many times that they finally manage to do it by themselves and without thinking — but this is a process requiring a lot of time and planning.

The Desire for Action Must be Kept Alive

At times, reality decrees that one should encourage the girls to use what they have, rather than teach a new skill or focus on improvement. One has to resort to whatever is available, for example, try to find the best use of the rhythmic arm and hand movements of the stereotypies.

It is often a question of finding out what arouses their motivation and then, drawing on this, to vary the situations so that the desire for action is kept alive. Perhaps a girl does not reach for anything except for an item that sparkles and gleams in the light of a flashlight in a dark room. Another one may find it exciting to tear away a scarf from the mirror, or wipe away foam from it, so that she can see herself again. Keep on trying! The most important thing is that the adult's eagerness to teach must not drive away the desire for action by refusing to accept what is "wrong," if this "wrong" is the girl's optimum ability in a given situation. The abilities and needs of the individual person must always be the starting point. It is essential that she experience success in whatever she does. If she achieves a result that is important to *her*, she will maintain a desire to repeat the action. Improvement comes with practice and consequently her actions will improve with time. When sufficiently improved, the action can be expanded by the addition of new elements.

Handedness

The potential for these girls to achieve satisfactory hand-motor skills is so small that it is imperative to focus on maintaining whatever skills there are. Emphasis should be put on taking advantage of what the girls do best.

This means that one has to identify the hand that possesses the desire for action. This hand should be used in all spontaneous situations, and the activity training should be concentrated on it. Some of the girls tend to switch hands, and if they themselves transfer the desire for action to the other hand, this must be noted and appropriate adjustments carried through. At times the desire for action is in the "inferior" hand. "Inferior" in this context usually implies that the hand used for grasping is not capable of maintaining the grip. The other hand, however, may be more capable of maintaining a hold, and so the adult is eager to teach the girl to use *that* hand for grasping. In those cases where handedness is not very marked, it may be possible to induce the "superior" hand to perform the grasping. My personal opinion is that the hand that reaches to grasp is still the "best" hand just because it already has the desire for action — and grasping comes before maintaining the grip. Compensating that hand for its poor ability to maintain a grip, by employing various aids, would, in my opinion, be a preferable method.

To eliminate such a desire for action and to try to awaken a new one is probably impossible in most cases, and the chance that the girl will act without desire is very slim. To switch hands because of external requests is difficult even for children without handicaps. It is even more difficult for those with Rett syndrome, as they already have a confused identity. However, in certain specific situations, where it would be practical for the girls to have an automatic movement, one may teach them to use the most "suitable" hand, independent of handedness. One can also encourage them to use their non-dominant hand for assistance, where this is suitable. All of them, after all, know that both hands can be used and that they may have different functions — a fact that is demonstrated over and over again by the girls themselves through their stereotypies.

Each Girl Requires Her Own Solutions

Using the hands is sometimes a roundabout way. The girls may be better able to achieve their goals by grasping with their eyes or mouth. There will be cases where the hands must be regarded as useless instruments and where one must look for something else for the girls to use.

Only someone who knows the girl well will be able to find out what works best for her. The ideas presented in this book are only examples. For each girl there will possibly be solutions suitable just for her. The starting point must be her own interests, abilities, and needs. In many cases, it would be advantageous to plan the course of action with an occupational therapist, who can also give advice concerning the design and adaptation of technical aids.

Various Attempts to Moderate the Hand Stereotypies

Not only do the hand mannerisms interfere with the girl's purposeful hand movements, but in addition, they can be obstructing and troublesome in other ways. For instance, it is very difficult to feed the girl if she constantly has her hands in her mouth. Mealtimes usually require special solutions. The stereotypies are often especially pro-nounced at mealtimes, since eating situations involve a complex mixture of positive and negative stresses. In addition, many girls themselves become frustrated by their hands going into their mouth, and thus the stress increases further.

The stereotypies not only increase with stress, but also increase when the girls are inactive and have nothing else to occupy their attention. Then the stereotypic hand movements in turn reinforce their self-absorption, and a vicious circle begins.

The stereotypies may also cause physical damage. For one thing, they may have an aggressive component, and for another the repeated contact between the hands and the mouth (or other parts of the body) can result in sores, swellings, rashes, and vomiting.

Consequently, it is desirable to find some means to moderate the stereotypies. Of course, attempts should be made to avoid inactivity and self-occupation, and stressful situations should also be avoided. This, however, is not always possible — and a complete avoidance of positive stress is in any case not desirable. Which method to use for moderating the stereotypies depends on the situation and the nature of the hand movements of the individual.

Physical Prompts. For an adult to hold the girl's hands is the most common and natural way of restraining her hand movements. This method works well, provided that it is only used in certain defined situations and that the girl herself is disturbed by the stereotypic movements and has something else to which she would rather devote her energy.

Verbal Prompts. Verbal correction is a simple, effective method which may, however, be difficult to put into practice. Verbal corrections can be extraordinarily effective if their aim is taught in a correct way — that is, saying "no" and removing the girls hands every time they go into her mouth, for instance. Both the words and the motion should come instantly and together, whenever she puts her fingers into her mouth, and they must present a signal sufficiently strong to be understood by her. Care should be taken not to scare her, but the signal must still have a negative impact; that is, she must experience it as something unpleasant which she will consequently avoid exposing herself to again.

Here too, of course, it is not feasible to prevent the stereotypies in this way except for specific situations. If one, from the beginning, defines certain situations, for example, mealtimes, where preventing the stereotypic movements are considered to be most important, the chances of success are considerably increased. It is important to be completely consistent in these situations. When the girl understands, a single "no" will suffice to stop the undesired behavior. If used sparingly, such a "no" can also be effective in some other situations. Used too often, it turns into nagging and will be ignored.

When a desirable behavior is established, it has to be maintained by continued watchfulness and prompts from the adult. If one does not carry through, there is always a risk that one may suddenly find oneself in a situation where the girl knows, but does not care — she undisturbedly persists in her hand movements.

This behavior may also result if the adult is not "sufficiently critical" in tone. The girl demonstrates that she has discovered an association between "no" and "hands away," but this association does not possess the true emotional value. Many people describe how the process of learning becomes a mere game. For instance, the girl does exactly what she is not supposed to do, in a very conscious manner. With sparkling eyes she raises her hands to her mouth, eagerly awaiting a reaction from the adult. The adult says "no." The girl perhaps lowers her hands slightly, then raises them again, while she in eager anticipation awaits the next "no." This game may be fun, but it is hardly effective for the intended purpose. It is, however, a charming example illustrating the girl's social and intellectual level. Not everybody is able to take the initiative to tease consciously in this manner.

Restraints. In subduing the stereotypies many parents find it easier to use various aids than to make their daughters obey verbal prompts. The simplest restraint may be a towel wrapped around the hand to prevent hand to mouth behavior. The towel will also lessen the risk of damage, if the hand still goes to the mouth. Some parents have used splints, braces, mittens, or water wings for the same purpose. No perfect aid has been found, however, that prevents the stereotypies without interfering with other hand functions. In order not to hamper the child unnecessarily, one could employ the restraints only at mealtimes when she is being fed and her hand movements are an interference. However, it is important that she does not perceive the eating situation as being negative. To help, but to help by hampering, is a method that should not be used too often. Other methods could be used for other daily routines.

Distractions. The hand mannerisms of the girls spontaneously decrease when the girls are sufficiently distracted by something else. Many parents report that the stereotypies diminish when their daughters are being "confused" or induced to "forget" about their hands.

The problem is finding a sufficient number of stimuli with sufficient duration in time. The stimuli have to be strong and intrusive, and place such a heavy demand on the girls' attention, that the stereotypies become a "disturbance." They must also be so varied and interesting that they manage to captivate the attention for a long span of time. Activities that serve well in these respects are those that stimulate muscular sense (especially movements engaging the whole body), sight, and hearing. The more senses that are activated concurrently, the better the activity will compete with the stereotypies, because the less scope the girls will have to spare. For instance, an engaging interaction with another person can occupy the girl to such an extent that her hand movements totally cease (or otherwise it is often natural in these situations to hold her hands without disturbing the girl). Playing with shades, flashlights, or candles, tracking soap bubbles, dancing, or engaging in action rhymes, looking at pictures, listening to stories or to someone sitting close by singing and playing an instrument, are activities that may block the stereotypies, though this does not always work. Watching a special TV program, riding in a car, or taking a walk are other attention-demanding activities.

When the girls are exposed to something new, exploring this new situation often places such an enormous demand on their senses that they have no time left for anything else. If such a situation is "just right" — which means, not frightening or stress-provoking by being so complex that the attention is shattered — it will sometimes have a moderating effect on the stereotypies, or at least alter their characteristics. For example, the rhythm will slacken or hands that are usually in the mouth might be held at chest level. However, note that there is always a risk that the opposite occurs — the girl's interest may turn into eagerness, provoking her to intensify her hand movements.

Stimulating Constructive Use of Hands. Distracting the girls, as described above, is a way to stimulate them by engaging them in other occupations. Of course, they can also be stimulated or distracted by the adult introducing different hand activities competing with the stereotypies. Such competition is created when the hands are engaged in something more interesting than the stereotypies, like playing finger games, or when the girls are urged to participate actively in eating finger food. One can also create situations where it is necessary to do something specific with the hands, like holding on to some kind of handle in order to maintain one's balance when going for a walk, riding on a horse, or jumping on a trampoline.

Significance of the Hand Stereotypies. Moderation of the hand movements may prove successful. They can also be completely neutralized at certain times. Eliminating or "forbidding" the hand movements totally does not seem to be possible. They must, for example, be permitted when they express happiness and eagerness. The movements are not governed by will power. They are a product of a compulsion which we know very little about. We can surmise that the stereotypies occur because, in some way, the hands feel "strange" and the movements relieve some of that feeling. Or the stereotypies may represent a way of channelling a need for motion, which has no normal outlet. Or maybe again, the brain governs the hands directly. Knowing the situation of the girls, one must also acknowledge the significance the stereotypies have in their lives. While their attempts to attain constructive hand function often end in failure, the stereotypies become movements trained to perfection. Nothing else has been practiced by the girls to the same extent. The hand mannerisms become something they girls can cope with and succeed in, even if they fail in everything else. In this way they will gradually increase in significance, motivating the girls to go on. Furthermore, if one constantly performs a gesture that behavior will finally become part of oneself, helping to build up an identity. Should the stereotypies cease, life would feel strange and wrong. One is no longer a complete person without that identifying factor. Whenever one attempts to moderate or break the hand movements, one's first consideration must always be the respect for the girl's own needs. Sometimes the hand movements can be disturbing to the girls themselves. At other times, they may act as a "shelter" or help the girls to tolerate anxiety. "It does not work to stop her completely," many parents say, "then she becomes unhappy." — "She needs to do it." — "If we hold her hands, she carries on with her tongue instead." — "When we let go of her hands, she is more active than ever, as if to make up for lost time." — "It is part of her life, of her." — "It is her way of knowing that here I am — I exist."

5 Interacting and Communicating with the Environment

Those with Rett syndrome do not have "normal" contacts with the environment, but they are not uninterested in people. On the contrary, they focus strongly on people in their environment. Still, their "contact radius" is rather limited. The girls may notice a person at a distance, but one must come very close to them in order to really awaken and sustain their interest. One must also find the "channel" to each particular girl, in order to create and develop contact with her.

Interest in establishing direct contact with the environment increases with time, as does the ability emotionally to express this interest. However, the inability of these girls in other ways to communicate with their surroundings still remains a severe handicap. This can be tremendously frustrating to them — they know what they want, but they are not able to make themselves understood. Nevertheless, many of the girls exert themselves to express their wishes, and they may become impatient and unhappy or frantic when they do not succeed, a despair that may result in violent temper tantrums or self-injurious behavior.

Reasons for Communication Difficulties

The inability to express their wishes depends on the girl's primary communication handicap, the verbal apraxia. But it is also a result of the interaction between this apraxia and the other handicaps, and of the girls' ability to handle their handicaps. The sensitivity of their surroundings is also of great importance.

Physical Handicaps. The girls' chances of making themselves understood are highly dependent on the degree of their physical handicap. Those who are ambulatory and have active hand motor skills have a big advantage. Should such a girl, for example, when in a shop, approach a clothes rack and repeatedly touch a pair of orange pants, thereby indicating that she wants them, she would have a good chance of getting them. In any event, she will attract attention, and her request will be properly interpreted. A girl in a wheelchair, on the other hand, who gazes with all her power at the same pants, does not have the same opportunity to have her desire heeded. But both girls try to send the same message, and they do express themselves clearly to the best of their respective abilities.

The Sensitivity of the Environment. The people whom these girls "talk" to must be prepared to interpret them, even if they are using their own individual and unusual signals, which we ordinarily are not trained to read. The more severe the girls' handicap, the greater is the sensitivity required from those around them. It is easy to forget that they have not lost their ability to want and choose, though they have lost the ability to express what they want in a conventional manner.

Self-Confidence. If the girls are never noticed or never succeed in getting their efforts in communicating interpreted, there is a risk that they may give up in their endeavors to transmit signals to the environment.
    Various methods must be applied to strengthen the girls' identity and self-esteem. Just as one can improve their understanding of their bodies, one can improve their self-awareness by, for example, mirror-games, songs, their own photo albums, series of slides, and tape recordings. It is also important to try to strengthen their understanding of their own abilities. If the environment views these girls as people without the will or power to do anything, they themselves will have no chance of creating a positive self-image or the self-confidence needed to take an active part in the world around them.

Methods of Communication

By paying attention to and reinforcing the girls' spontaneous signals, one can eventually reach an "agreement" where the girls know that if they express themselves in a certain way, they will obtain a response from their environment. The environment in turn is attuned to a certain "channel of communication," and knows what to look for.

Even a form of behavior that originally may be random, rather than intended as a signal — an instinctive expression of a need or a desire — can, through consistent reinforcement, be transformed into purposeful communication.

It may work like this: a girl may express a wish to drink by fixing her eyes on her glass on the table. If nothing happens, she may look from her glass to the adult. If she still gets no attention, she may resort to screaming in a demanding way. If this method also fails, she may try to grasp the glass. This she is unable to do, and the glass, as well as other objects in her way, are tipped over and perhaps fall to the floor. If she is still able to concentrate on her wish, in the general commotion, and still does not get a drink, she may start to cry and bite her hands.

Depending on at what stage the adult steps in and responds, one of these actions will be reinforced. If this is repeated consistently a sufficient number of times, a method of communication can eventually be established where the girl and the listener both know what "language" each is to use.

No signal can be said to be more correct than another (but of course one should not force the girls to despair!). The signal, or the combination of signals to be selected in the case in question depend on the girl's ability, the particular circumstances, and the environment's willingness and ability to interpret her. In each unique case, one should try to find out what the girl's natural resources are. Likewise, her needs and her abilities will dictate which signals to use when addressing her.

Words and Sounds. Speech as a form of communication is not possible for these girls. Their vocalizations and their few words can often be drawn out and intensified by the adults imitating and replying to them, or by letting the girls listen to their own voices on a tape recorder. Many valuable instances of contact and "dialogue" can be created in this manner, but hardly a way of conveying messages. However, if one can think of some way to teach the girls to vocalize to gain attention, or to use their sounds as a complement to other communication methods, a lot will have been gained. For instance, if the girl in the wheelchair, who wanted a pair of orange pants, had been able to vocalize, she would have been more likely to gain attention than when she was only using her eyes.

Music cannot be used as a means of communication in the conventional way, but it still paves the way to an interaction with these patients. Music often awakens their interest in their surroundings, and with the help of music therapy they can participate in a "dialogue," where they alternately listen and answer.

Gestures and Signs. It is natural to resort to words when explaining something to the girls. In the same manner, gestures and signs are natural complements when addressing them. At times, one can use simple signs which the girls will catch with their eyes. At other times, their arms or hands can be moved to enable them to understand the sign with their entire body.

Because the girls lack motor skills, it is much more difficult to induce them to use gestures and signs. In some exceptional cases, some girls use spontaneous gestures in a special situation — for example, they will lead the hand to the mouth when they are thirsty or pat the diaper when it is wet. These gestures, however, often become diffuse movements, which conceal themselves in the girls' stereotypies and, as a result, become very hard to detect and interpret by those around them. In practice, they have a very limited application.

Ambulatory girls can show what they want by merely moving about. They can approach that which they want and perhaps also touch it to make clear what they mean. Many girls do not possess this ability and are severely restricted by the limits of their geographical reach. Girls with Rett syndrome ordinarily do not point to objects, but they can hit them or reach for them, if they are close enough and the girls assess them to be within reach.

Vocalization and motor skills are both dependent on the patterns of fluctuations and thus are often unreliable as the only types of signals from the girls.

Eye-Pointing. There are times when the girls seem to be in a temporary "down spell," where their vocalizations cease and their movements taper off, and their interest in the world around them and the desire to communicate with it both seem to be low. Even during these periods, however, they continue to take in the world with their eyes, and they use the eyes to transmit signals. Furthermore, since their visual range is more extensive than their body range, and since they grasp better with their eyes than with their hands, their eyes become a natural tool of communication. They acquire information through their eyes, "talk" through their eyes, show feelings, express what they want, ask and seek confirmation through their eyes.

Often, the best way to establish a method of communication is to systematically encourage the girls' eye-pointing; especially in those cases where the girls are severely disabled. This, however, places heavy demands upon those around the girls when it comes to sensitivity and willingness to interpret. It also requires workable arrangements. If the girls are going to be able to express their wishes through eye-pointing, that which they want must in some way be visible to them.

Well-defined situations can be simplified by giving the girls an opportunity to choose. For instance, at the dinner table a girl may select what to drink, from alternatives placed in front of her. In the same way she can enjoy deciding which sweater she prefers, which book she wants to look at, or which record she wants to listen to.

But, to anticipate a situation, and indicate what one wants, one has to be in the "right" place. In the kitchen area one may, for example, indicate thirst by looking at a glass or at the faucet. In the living room, and sitting in a wheelchair, it is harder to express the need for a drink of water. On the other hand, it is easier to express a wish to listen to the stereo in the living room than in the kitchen. When the girls are in the "wrong" place they can become bored, unhappy, or angry, or in some other way show that they want something they cannot express. When the adult applies the trial-and-error method to ascertain what a girl wants, and does not succeed, it is hard to know whether this depends on the girl's lack of understanding or on the adult's guesses being incorrect.

Tangible Symbols. When the girls are in the "wrong" place one can use various kinds of symbols to help them to explain themselves. In the schools, tangible symbols are commonly used as complements to words, signs, etc. when the girls are given information about something that is going to happen. This is partly because one does not know how well they understand words, and partly because a tangible object serves as a more lasting stimulus — an advantage when dealing with those who are easily distracted and whose reactions are delayed. A spoon can be used as a symbol for "now it is time to eat food," a diaper for "now it is time to go to the bathroom," the girl's cap for "now it is time to go outside," or her school bag for "now it is time to go home." Of course, such tangible symbols can also be used to give the girls a chance to show what they themselves want, as a guide to those around them. In situations where it is clear that the girls want something, a number of well-known symbols to choose from might be presented to them as a reinforcement to verbal questions.

Pictures. Using symbols will be considerably simplified if the girls can read pictures. As mentioned before, many people point out that these girls understand pictures and that many of them can interpret both familiar and unfamiliar pictures.

In school it is not unusual to use pictures instead of or in conjunction with tangible symbols in order to give information or to prepare the girls for what is about to occur. However, pictures are not used to give information in as many situations as might be expected, considering the fact that so many people do believe that the girls understand pictures, and that so many of us are uncertain how well they understand words. It is also unusual to use pictures, and tangible symbols as well, with the opposite purpose — that is, to allow the girls to show what they themselves want by direct selection. This is probably partly due to the traditional educational view — it is the adult who transmits information to the student. To prepare the students for what is about to happen is, in addition, a means of reducing anxiety, and the importance of doing this is perfectly clear to most people who work with the girls.

The inability to understand the girls is considered to be a major problem for those working with them as well as for the girls themselves, but at the same time there is considerable uncertainty concerning how to tackle this problem. The explanation of this is surely that the task of finding an appropriate method of communication is so difficult, that the teachers require support and help in their efforts. This type of assistance is available to very few of them. Only a couple of teachers have had access to consultations with speech therapists to discuss these girls.

Only two girls in the sample used pictures as a means of expressing a need or desire. The introduction of such methods had, however, been considered in several cases and in some cases was also planned to be introduced. One of the girls who does use pictures to tell what she wants has a communication board with a picture in each corner. The pictures symbolize "eat," "drink," "go to the toilet," and "rest." If the girl wishes to do one of these things, she manages to make a little sound to get attention. Then the board is fetched and she looks at the picture that represents her wish. This girl, now and then, also manages to move her hand towards the picture in question. She is very happy and proud when she is able to make herself understood, and to thus get a chance to do what she wants. The intention, of course, is to equip the communication board with additional pictures, chosen to suit this particular girl.

In order to enable the girls to use pictures for communication, they must first have an opportunity to learn what the different pictures represent. The picture and the object or situation it symbolizes must be presented together and repeatedly a sufficient number of times to make the association quite clear, before one can expect a girl herself to use the picture as a symbol. When she has really understood the principle that a picture represents something real, then it will be easier to present new pictures to her, in order to explain something to her as well as to expand her active "vocabulary."

Since those with Rett syndrome are very clever at making quick associations in situations which they find important or take delight in, communication through pictures might prove to be a practical tool for many of them. The skill in making associations could possibly be used even among those girls who do not read pictures. Here one might arrange a set of symbols to select from on the basis of colors and forms, instead of using pictures depicting objects or situations. For example: green=food, red=toilet, or blue=listen to music.

When deciding which level to start from and how to establish a communication system for the girls, one should have the opportunity to consult a speech therapist. The therapist can also recommend what type of pictures should be used in each particular case — photographs of the girl herself in different situations, photo symbols, drawings, or abstract pictures like "Bliss." In some cases, a simple data technique could be used. The eye-pointing may need to be supported by gestures or by letting the girl point with directed light beams from a lamp fixed to her forehead or her glasses.

Communication Is Interaction

Many of these girls and women are so handicapped that they may not succeed in attaining a communication system where specific signals are used. Nevertheless, it is important that they gain attention through the means of expression they do have — visible signs of emotions, sounds, body tensions, or the intensity of the stereotypies — and that those around them are sensitive in theirs attempts to interpret them. Here too, it is often possible to respond to the girls in time to prevent temper tantrums and self-injury, which are painful to the girls themselves and upsetting to their caregivers as well. Communication is interaction — the "talker" as well as the "listener" must both play an active part, if the message is going to come through. Most of those with Rett syndrome will never be able to communicate in such a way that they will be understood by everybody. They will remain dependent upon "interpreters;" people close to them who know them so well, that they are able to "sense" whenever the girls cannot express their needs or preferences clearly enough.

6 Being Active

The girls' level of activity depends on the possibilities available for acting. Their failure to act might easily be mistaken for a lack of desire. However, if they are going to have any chance to act at all, one must grab hold of their actual desire, and use this desire as a basis try to find ways to compensate for their inability. Excessive passivity can be a question of obstacles within the girls themselves or in their environment. These obstacles can be physical as well as mental or emotional in nature.

Obstacles for Acting

Handicaps Within the Girls Themselves. The girls' understanding of their environment may be too poor for them to have any desire or possibility of actively participating. Perhaps they feel that they can have no effect on their surroundings, or reach any goals through their own actions. Another impediment might be an insufficient ability to sense and use their bodies.

Obstacles in the Environment. There are cases where it may seem impossible to compensate the girls for their handicaps. Perhaps there is a lack of understanding of the real nature of their handicaps, or one simply does not know what to do. Perhaps the girls have difficulties not even noticed, and consequently proper steps cannot be taken to help them.

The adults may also misjudge the children's behavior. Perhaps the girls *are* active (for example, watching something, or in some other way taking in a situation) but they are not judged by their own capacity for activity, but by other people's idea of what activity is. In order for the girls to participate in play and daily activities such as eating or dressing, the interaction between them and their environment must work without unnecessary obstacles. Those situations set aside for the girls to participate in must meet their abilities as well as their level of motivation.

Starting from the Girls' Abilities

Structured Situations. Before the girls can be expected to act in a particular situation they have to understand that situation. They must be familiar with it or feel secure in it. They must also understand their own role in the situation, either from previous experience or from intuitive insight. The required aids must be available. The situation must also be designed to help them in their perceptual and cognitive difficulties. For example, a girl cannot be expected to distinguish her own towel from many others, if one does not in some way mark it out for her. To help her, one can place it on a separate rack; or put a photo of herself above it; or let her towel be red if the others are blue.

Consideration of the Girls' Own Actions. It is impossible to determine from without what "should" be enjoyable to the girls, and just as impossible to determine what they "should" be able to do. One must always start with the particular individual's efforts and encourage the response she gives rather than ask for what she does not give. The girl, herself, must be allowed to decide how she will respond. Possibly, her way is better than the response imagined by the adult. If one encourages what is already there and increases the demands by degrees, the responses may eventually become clearer and stronger. In time, a wider range of responses may evolve.

Perhaps one wants the girl to grasp an object. She might start with grasping with her eyes only. Or one may want a sound from her, but she just tenses all the muscles in her body. Her response is not the desired one, but the fact that she did respond is the first step, no matter how feeble the response may be.

Allow for Time. Adapting the situation to the girls' needs also means giving them the time they require. It is important to remember that they often have delayed response reactions. Perhaps they need a long time to assess a situation and adjust to it before the desire to participate arises. Maybe, too, a span of time will be required between wanting to act and really being able to. The environment can assist, but it is the girls themselves who know when they are ready to act.

The quality of their concentration must be understood, and the conditions arranged so that the situation is "still there" when they are "ready." A good example is the girl who was requested to blow out a candle during the morning circle in school. She recognized the situation, understood it, and the teacher was reasonably sure that she knew what was expected of her. However, the girl did not show in any conventional manner that she had understood or had the desire to perform the task. She looked away, breathed hard, wriggled her body, rolled up her eyes, and intensified her hand movements. Thanks to the patient waiting of the people around her, the candle was still in front of her when after a while she suddenly leaned forward and exhaled so that the flame was extinguished.

There are difficulties in establishing a dialogue with these girls as there is with many multihandicapped persons. These difficulties occur because "normal" people are not accustomed to the drastically different tempo. One has to be very slow and at the same time very quick to accommodate to these individuals. They must have a sufficient length of time in order to act and the environment must passively wait, yet remain actively alert. When the girls finally do act, the environment must in turn be very quick and active in its affirmation, to reinforce the response and encourage repetition.

Often, situations occur when there is no interaction or "dialogue" though all conditions exist. The reaction time is so slow that the adult has already "moved on" and does not understand — or even notice — the response when it comes. This in turn can be incomprehensible and confusing to the girls and lead to reactions misinterpreted by the adult as being unreasonable and bizarre.

Opportunity for Repetitions. There is also another aspect of time involved. Since all their movements become smoother when their activity has been going on for a while, and since learning also takes place as a result of repeated experiences, it is a good idea to design situations where the girls are given the opportunity to repeat an activity or to keep on with it for a while. Sometimes, for example, it is better to take a longer walk than one that is too short. From this point of view, it may also be better to connect a switch to a slide projector rather than to a tape recorder. While the music continues to play once the tape recorder has been activated, the projector requires repeated operation of the switch to change the scenery. The strain involved in concentrating and then performing a task causes many of these girls to tire quickly. This does not necessarily mean that their interest has diminished. Some have "quiet spells" when the activity is changed into periods of rest and contemplation. They appear to "tune out," and they actually do, but it is a very natural response for them. They need their time for recuperation and processing. When given a little time, the girls respond again and with renewed vigor. My own student often requires these rest periods. Note that some of the girls with epileptic seizures have quiet spells where a real mental absence occurs, not a mere lapse.

Protection Against Distractions. In order for the girls to hold their concentration and have the opportunity to act, they must be protected against distracting incidents, which threaten not only to break but also to misdirect their attention. Those stimuli that are most enjoyable, such as moving lights, sounds, and signals from their own bodies, also catch the attention at the "wrong" moments and divert attention from the original situation. A sudden sound, a sunray, a patterned tablecloth, a curtain flickering in the wind, hands moving forward on a clock's face, wet diapers, the smell of food — almost anything can create a disturbance at the wrong moment. If the girls' concentration is broken, it may take time to reestablish it. If this occurs several times in a row, and if their attention is not recaptured successfully by the "right" task, the whole undertaking may become tiresome and something in which they would rather not participate. Often it is not possible to remove all imaginable distractions but it could make a great difference in which room, or in which part of the room, the girl is asked to perform a task.

Starting from the Girls' Own Motivation

It is the girls' motivation; that is, their own inner driving force, that will enable them to "overcome themselves," and in some exceptional situations perform tasks that prove that their inability is not total. It is rather a matter of their having a very "selective" ability.

Attempts to motivate them only from without will very seldom be successful. Such attempts may rather lead to further blockage if the adult appeals to "wrong" channels. One should instead try to find and reinforce their inner motivation and find situations which are pleasant in themselves, and where the girls' actions lead to results that are meaningful to them.

Sphere of Interest. If the adults are to be able to create situations enticing the girls to act, a thorough knowledge of the individual girl and an understanding of her sphere of interest is required.

The sphere of interest of the girls in my study was pretty narrow. Most of them also had similar interests, regardless of age and stage of disorder. Maybe this is because these interests reflect things that everybody, even severely handicapped people, can frequently take part in and gain many experiences from.

These girls usually like bodily contact, both cuddling and rough play. They generally like bathing and swimming, listening to singing and music, watching TV, looking at books, and listening to stories. They like being outdoors, riding in a car, or being walked in a wheelchair. They like children, especially toddlers and babies. They like familiar photos, pictures of certain people and of food. They seldom have favorite toys apart from dolls and music boxes. As mentioned previously, there are certain visual stimuli that especially capture their interest, and most of them love food.

It is within their own range of interests that those with Rett syndrome are active, both in terms of communication and action. If they are judged below their true level, it is often due to the fact that those around them have not given sufficient consideration to the girls' own world and the things they understand and enjoy. One cannot expect them to respond to something that holds no meaning for them.

Motivating by Creating Anticipation. Starting from the girls' own interests, one can try to create situations where their own active participation feels meaningful and necessary to them.

Building up anticipation when playing with a girl is one way of stimulating her, if this anticipation is so strong that she has to "realize" it. A lack of balance is created, which in turn creates a longing for balance. A well-known song could, for instance, be broken off prematurely, and since the girls generally know it is not finished, they will probably indicate this knowledge one way or another. The music therapist works in much the same way, by creating and relieving tension and excitement.

Starting from familiar everyday routines is another way of motivating the girls in this manner. If a girl is aware of how an activity starts, progresses and concludes, she has the opportunity to participate — if she is given the chance. Perhaps she enjoys washing her hands, for instance, with her own funny soap. Then she probably knows that after the water is turned on, her hands get wet and then it is time to soap them. If, some day, the nice soap is just lying there and no one soaps her hands with it, she has the chance of doing something herself, (whine or look at or reach for the soap), and show that she knows what is going to happen, even if she will need help to perform it.

To use routines in this way, and to provoke the girls to act by interrupting a familiar pattern of behavior, is a method that can be used in all kinds of situations. In this way anticipation is created, an expectation of continuation and completion. When the completion is threatened the girls are driven to act. It becomes *their* responsibility to force the operation forwards. Gradually their own performance may become part of the routine.

Each family surely can find situations where their daughter could have a chance to act in this manner. It can be a question of taking off her cap, shaking loose her arm from the coat, opening the water faucet, or turning on the light. Examples that clearly demonstrate how the girls showed anticipation were reported from 32 of the 39 girls in the sample. In 20 of these cases, one could also give examples of how they actively tried to move the operation forward.

Often, such situations occur without deliberate planning. In one way or another, a pause may occur in a normal chain of events, and is so long that the girl becomes impatient. A common situation is when the adult talks to another adult at the table and forgets to feed the child. Then perhaps, for the first time, she takes hold of the adult's arm. This is a reaction that, with a little alertness from the adult, could be formed into a routine where the girl actively participates in the feeding without being able to perform the entire action herself. Holding on to the adult's arm/hand, and following the entire movement from plate to mouth and back again teaches the arm motion that is the beginning of "feeding oneself." (For many girls, this pattern is easier to accept than the adult hand-over-hand helping them to hold the spoon themselves.) This also gives her the important experience of being an active participant in a situation.

Of course, provocation by the adults deliberately forgetting to complete a process does not always work. The girl may have a very slow reaction time and become distracted on her way to action, or perhaps there is no time to wait for her getting ready to act. Perhaps she does not understand the situation fully, or perhaps it is not pleasant enough for her to want a continuation. Or perhaps she may just have a "bad" day.

The process is one of balance, in which the girl must be given a chance to act on her own while the adult waits for her — but, if she cannot act, the waiting time must not be so long that she despairs of completion and chooses to withdraw from the situation. If, for whatever reason, she cannot act on her own, the adult has to act in her place and let her try again another time when the conditions are different.

To Be a Participant. Many of these girls, with their severe handicaps, will always have a small behavior repertoire, despite their own exertions as well as those of their environment. But what is meant by "small" also depends on how words like "action" and "active performance" are defined. I think it is essential to realize that action is not always something that can be observed and not always what we ordinarily perceive as action. One can be just as active when taking in an experience as when acting outwards. For girls with Rett syndrome, watching may sometimes be a very active and fully significant action. And there are occasions where a raising of the head or a conscious exhalation, if emanating from the girl herself, are worth a lot more, even if they are less obvious, than, for instance, an arm movement that is fully executed with the help of the adult, without any physical or emotional participation from the girl.

Even when acting, these girls are always dependent on the interaction with their environment. Mostly, their acting requires interpretation and help from the environment before an action can be completed. A child with Rett syndrome cannot, for example, take her coat and go outside independently, but she might start a chain of actions by going out in the hallway and touching her coat.

Given the chance to do what they can do, the girls will gain the precious experience of participation, regardless of how little they actually can perform. Too few and too small demands can make them unhappy, as can too many and too great demands. Being understimulated — never to need or to have a chance to do anything — may likewise produce passivity, withdrawal, intense hand action, or self-injurious behavior.

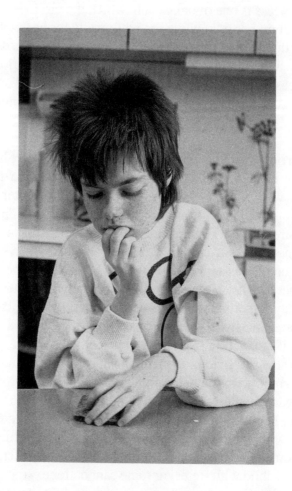

*Ulrika cannot hold a spoon by herself. However, she can try to grasp
pieces of bread and fruit. Note that she is left-handed. This size of rye-
crisp is adaptable to her grasp. Rye-crisp is appropriate because it
does not slip out of her grasp too easily. If Ulrika's hands are sticky
from saliva, she has an even better grip. The rye-crisp is harder to
manage if buttered. If butter is wanted, soft bread is better, because
it remains in the hand when being squeezed.*

Ulrika manages to keep her eyes fixed on the bread. She also manages to finally grasp it and maintain her hold. The rhythmic movements of her hand are helpful in this case by allowing the bread further into her hand. Frequently the movements work in the opposite way, and Ulrika loses the bread before she has lifted her hand from the table.

Ulrika is concentrating hard, and she knows what she wants. Still, success is uncertain. Her hand stereotypies threaten to take over all the time, so that the left hand drops the bread and begins scratching the right hand instead, when the hands get close to each other. Also the bread can fall from her grasp if the hand opens at the same time as the mouth.

This time Ulrika is successful. She gets the bread up to the mouth, into the mouth, and takes a bite. She does not remove her right hand from the mouth, until just before the bread in her left hand is going to enter Not until then is she able to ease her concentration and look at us again, satisfaction in her eyes. Soon Ulrika will again be waving her hand in stereotypic movements, the bread falling from her hand, and the entire procedure must be repeated before the next bite of bread.

7 Expanding One's World

Regardless of age, those with Rett syndrome behave in many ways like small children; in their actions as well as in the way they learn new things. We take it as quite normal for a small child to want to do something in spite of not being able to, or become furious when he/she fails to perform a task or to explain something to an adult. Neither are we concerned about small children looking instead of talking, using the mouth instead of the hands, being fascinated by certain visual stimuli, being in many ways uncoordinated and unmodulated, having difficulties in controlling body and feelings, exhibiting sudden switches between laughter and tears, being able to perform only one task at a time, and needing concentration for success. These behaviors are natural parts of a child's development, appearing naturally at certain age levels. The problem is that the girls with Rett syndrome, regardless of age, remain at this level of functioning. The behavior they display is often similar to that of a child 12—18 months old. They are not just "ill" — there is also the question of functions being prevented from maturing due to this illness.

Learning

Due to all their interacting and complicated handicaps, these individuals have difficulty in progressing to "higher" learning levels. They learn nothing from conscious imitation, but must focus on the sensation from their own bodies when learning a movement. Their ability to generalize and to carry out abstract reasoning is limited. They will always be dependent on tangible and concrete experiences to fully understand a situation. They have difficulty in translating and adjusting their knowledge to entirely new situations, but have to learn one situation at a time in order to act in an appropriate way. They are dependent on their own inner driving force, for acting as well as for learning, and they cannot alleviate a waiting process by reasoning. They have to have certain "cues," otherwise they require immediate satisfaction of their needs.

This does not mean that these girls cannot learn new things. They can and they do. They continuously expand their understanding of themselves and their environment, and they can learn to perform better and with greater security and confidence. But they reach their understanding in certain ways. They learn "in width" instead of "in height" — that is, they learn how to act in a wider range of situations instead of learning skills that are more and more difficult. Their level of abstraction continues to be low, and the learning principles they have to follow restrict their learning to that which is tangible and concrete, frequently repeated, and experienced through their senses and with strong emotional feelings.

"Frequently repeated," in this context, really means repeated *many* times. All of us have to practice many times before a movement works perfectly, for instance. If you are handicapped you will have to practice still more before you reach a satisfactory level of performance. Furthermore, you cannot create the training situations yourself, but those around you will have to do it for you.

If the behavior repertoire of the girls is to be expanded, one will have to start out from their own sphere of interest and perhaps also expand this sphere by making more things, people, and situations meaningful to them. Likewise, if their level of activity is to be raised, one must try to raise their degree of interest.

The Starting Point for Teaching

Where to put the priority in each individual case depends on the strengths and weaknesses of the girl in question, and of her frame of reference and her system of values. The starting point should always be the girl herself, what she *can* do, what she *wants*, and what she *needs*.

This also means that one must adjust one's priorities to the different stages of the illness. In the second stage of the illness, when everything crumbles and the child's world turns into chaos, it is first and foremost a question of rebuilding her sense of security and the orderliness of her world. The training to regain lost abilities may have to be put on hold for a while, until the girl again opens up to her surroundings and is ready to participate in active training.

Everybody familiar with these girls knows that they have their "good" and "bad" days, and that consideration must be given to this fact. Assigning priorities according to the situation of the individual also entails giving consideration to the amount of experiences she has acquired. While it might be fun for the younger girl to play peek-a-boo games in front of a mirror, it might be more motivating for an older one to engage in hairdressing tasks. Likewise, the choice of pictures displayed will depend on the age of the child. For a little girl, one would choose to show her pictures representing familiar and well-known objects, whereas more complicated situation pictures could be selected for an older girl.

It should also be considered that advancing age and progression of the disorder make many of these girls tire easily. However, generally they tire more often from want of stimulation than from correctly prescribed and adapted stimulation.

The Learning Situation

I have previously covered the girls' various handicaps and their consequences in daily life, as well as the various adaptive measures required from a supportive environment. The importance of eliminating different kinds of disturbances has also been stressed.

In practice this means that often one ought to be alone with the girl in teaching situations or in a situation that is demanding or difficult in some other way. Most individuals in the study, in school or in daycare centers, have the opportunity for one-to-one instruction. The girl being alone with an adult in a "clean" environment does not entail just the elimination of possible distractions. She is also given the closeness required, spatially and emotionally. In this way she will be assured of the undivided attention of the adult, and this is a necessary condition for optimum interaction.

I want to underscore a fact that applies in all situations: the girls' physical and mental well-being is always the most important consideration and a prerequisite for enabling them to progress. None of us can succeed, whether we are processing information from the outside world or responding to it, if we do not feel well. If one has a general difficulty in performing, (as those with Rett syndrome do), this could cause one not to be able to do anything at all, unless one feels perfectly safe and physically comfortable. "Small" things, like itching, wrinkled clothing, clothes that rub or are too tight, uncomfortable sitting positions, or a tired back, feet swinging without support, a hungry or upset stomach, wet diapers, lack of sleep, pre- or post-seizure effects, etc. can be as distracting and disturbing as lights or sounds, and are furthermore in no way fascinating to the girls, but just unpleasant. Everything that interferes with the physical well-being also impedes the intellectual process.

Contribution of Specialists

These girls need an educational program that not only addresses isolated functions, but also involves an appropriate attitude to the entire individual, an attitude which creates favorable conditions for development and learning.

Girls with Rett syndrome are so multihandicapped that their teachers will need various kinds of support in this work.

The role of the physical therapists is obvious. They are responsible for physical training and technical aids, and can also initiate special activities like swimming and horseback riding.

The occupational therapist's knowledge is sometimes needed to find individual solutions and aids in relation to the girls' hand function.

Speech trainers and therapists ought to be the obvious consultants when trying to find forms of alternative communication.

Many of the teaching staff in my study also expressed a wish for pure educational guidance, and for support in gaining understanding of the conditions of the individual student. Those who worked with the more mobile group of girls requested more psychological guidance.

Music Therapy

As previously mentioned, music is a valuable aid for many of the girls. Music can be used in many different ways — in play, as accompaniment and props to everyday routines, as a support to verbal information. In addition, music is a joy in itself, and also an unfailing tool for opening up dialogue.

Moreover, there is music therapy, something which can be of great assistance to many of the multihandicapped. For these girls, who are so rhythmic, so audio-minded, so emotional, and who in many ways perceptually function on that deep level of consciousness where music, too, has its roots, music therapy should be still more valuable. Only a few of the girls with Rett syndrome in Sweden, however, have access to music therapy, despite the fact that this therapy could benefit all of them.

Through music therapy, the girls' inner desires and abilities can be captured. The music therapist creates "curves of excitement" — states of imbalance which must be resolved through the girls' own actions, based on their natural inherent desire for balance.

Thanks to the different senses supporting each other, the girls gain experiences through their own bodies that teach them about the world and about themselves. Through music therapy, they *feel*, and in this way come to understand, such concepts as time and space, quality and quantity, cause and effect. Their own identity is developed, too, and they will have better opportunities for acting, both when it comes to their skills and interaction with their surroundings. Though the girls require various kinds of specialized help, this does not mean that they must have it all at the same time. The aim must always be the optimum level of their well-being, not making their world muddled and fragmentary. In this connection, too, one must weigh the pros and cons, and set priorities in order to attain the most favorable situation for the individual girl.

Cooperation and Contact Between the Girls' Separate Environments

Even without specialist help, the girls will meet many people in their various separate environments. In order for the girls to feel comfortable, these people must understand them and know how to interpret them. In order to maximize the chances of correct interpretations of the girls' behavior, one has to know them well, see them over a long period of time, and in many situations. This means that there should not be more than the necessary personnel around each girl, and if possible the same personnel over a long period of time. When there are changes in the staff, good communication between the old and new personnel is necessary, preferably by their working side by side for some time. Each new person certainly can find new qualities in the girls, and also provide unique stimulation for them, but it is unnecessary to repeat each other's mistakes.

It is also important to establish contact between the girls' different separate environments in order to make it easier for all concerned to understand what the girls have experienced and promote a better interpretation of their behavior. This contact can be in the form of a verbal dialogue, written information in a special "contact book," where those around the girls can write notes to each other about what has happened during the day, or it can be a person following them from one environment to another. In this way one can also talk to the girls about their experiences, even if one did not participate, and thus help them to connect their different environments with each other, making them exist for the girls even when not here. A photo album in school with pictures showing the child's family and home, or a tape or a video recorded in school, describing a day or a happening there, and making it possible to later relive it at home, are other examples of how to connect the separate environments.

Social Contacts

The girls' emotional and social development is at least as important as intellectual and motor stimulation. They need other children; non-handicapped as well as handicapped. They may not be capable of playing with their peers, or of doing the same things, but they do derive great joy from being among them, watching their activities. Those girls who have severe motor handicaps also require help from adults in order to get physically close to other children — especially if these children, too, are disabled — to feel them and touch them.

I think that they also need to meet other children similar to themselves, such as other girls with Rett syndrome. In some of the classes I visited there were two girls with Rett syndrome in the same class. In one case they had a very close and special contact. The contact did not look like a conventional one, but the girls chose each other and actively sought each other's companionship. They would move close and cast furtive glances at one another and intensify their stereotypies while smiling to themselves.

However, this is not to say that one can generally recommend that those with Rett syndrome should make up a special class in school. Here, like elsewhere, it must be what the students have in common that decides the grouping. The girls in the case above were close to each other in age as well as in type and stage of disorder. In other cases, two girls could be of the same age, but so different that they would have more in common with other categories of students than with each other.

POSTSCRIPT

6

If we want to help those with Rett syndrome, we need to know what they find difficult, and also where their capabilities lie. This report is an attempt to describe these things and suggest which educational consequences such an analysis of the girls' situation may lead to.

No medical cure for the disorder has yet been discovered. Nor can therapy and teaching transform the girls into something they are not — only help to better use what they have.

Those with Rett syndrome will always be dependent on their environment — there they live, and there they may come across obstacles or find help to grow and develop. Development starts with interacting with other human beings, and just as the needs and behaviors of each individual girl must be analyzed, so must the conditions of her environment — and these conditions may have to be altered.

The important thing is to focus on what the girls can do, not on what they cannot, or do not, do. It is also important understand that ability is not only that which can be measured by external achievements — ability is everything that exists within, whether it can be expressed or not. The aim must be for the girl to use her abilities better, but this aim must be defined to suit her own needs, not to meet our needs of seeing her demonstrate those abilities.

My purpose with this book has been to share a way of thinking which I believe is crucial to working with multihandicapped people:

to let one's thinking find its starting point within the person concerned, and not in the exterior world that we have chosen as a standard. How we judge another person is just a matter of judgement. The score obtained is dependent on the measure used. This is something experienced by everyone close to these girls.

I will conclude with a poem, written by the mother of the very first girl in Sweden diagnosed as having Rett syndrome.

Wrong Judgement
My beloved child
You, who, although grown up
Need a helping hand
Always dependent on others
Let me whisper in your ear
Though you cannot understand
"You give me so much"

Capacity
Intelligence
Strength
Talent
We often judge so incorrectly
If you could only know what
Your laughing look just now
Gave me of joy and strength to go on

(Inga Wesslund 1984)

APPENDICES

7

1 Questions Forming a Basis for Interviews with Parents

Girl's Name _____ Age _____

Case history
What caused the parents to think there was something abnormal about the girl's development?
How old was the girl at that time?
Was the onset of the disorder insidious and gradual or sudden/unexpected?

At what age did the girl come to a standstill or a decline in her development?
What abilities disappeared?
How did the girl react to losing her abilities?

Was she for some period of time extremely anxious, uneasy or screaming?
Was she for some period of time withdrawn, not responding to contact?
Was she for some period of time hyperactive?
Was she for some period of time aggressive and/or self injurious?
Was there any trigger factor to the onset of the disorder?

Was the girl's development quite normal up to the first suspicion?
Were there even earlier delays or problems of any kind?
Breast fed until?
Any feeding problems (refusing the breast, bad sucking, vomiting, refusing solid food)?

Weight development
Problems of the stomach (vomiting, colic, constipation, air swallowing)

Sleeping problems (slept unusually much/little, abnormal day/night rhythm)

Gross motor development (sitting, crawling, pulling to a stand, walking — how? when?)

Hand-motor development (grasp, pincer grasp — how, when, unusual hand movements?)
Temperament (spells of screaming/laughter, extremely quiet)

Contact and interaction (eye contact, smiling, anticipation, affection, imitation)

Speech and language (babbling, deviant babbling, words)

Hearing

Sight

Playing

Infections, allergic problems, vaccinations, disorders

Special traumas (e.g., hospital stay, accidents, separations)

Today's situation
Changes (for the better/worse)

What are the greatest difficulties?

What is most important to the girl, in the parents' opinion?

Respite care, what kind, how much, want of more?

Can the girl be left alone?

Are there any problems taking her to shops, restaurants, public transports?

What are the effects on the social life of the family?

Reactions from siblings

Handling vacations and school holidays
Need of support/advice/information

Special problems and requirements

2 Questions Forming a Basis for Interview with Parents/Care Givers

Girl's name _____ Age _____

Degree of motor activity
Variations

Gross Motor Skills

Balance

Reactions to changes of position

Reactions to motor stimulation

Lying down
Can turn, how?
Can sit up
Can pull to stand

Sitting with/without support
Can raise to standing position, how?
Has been able to
Equilibrium reactions, protective response reactions

Standing with/without support
Broad based
Equilibrium reactions, protective response reactions
Can bend and pick objects from the floor
Can sit down (has been able to)

Crawling, how?
Position of hands/feet
Any asymmetries?

Standing on all fours
Kneeling

Walking with/without support
Way of walking
Need of initial help
Looks out where she is going
When did she learn to walk?
Any changes in ability

Not walking
Never been able to
Ambulatory for some period of time, when? Wheelchair bound, when?

Running, how?

Climbing stairs, how?

With/without support

Up/down

Reactions to obstacles

Real versus imaginary obstacles

Peculiar movements (trembling, shaking, rocking)
In what situations?

Physical therapy
Previous and present

Aids

Hand Motor Skills

Handedness

What can she do with her hands?

Changes

Grasping, how (palmar, finger grasp, pincer grasp)
Can hold objects
Can release her hold voluntarily
Can throw objects
Can move an object from one hand to another
Can bang objects on a table, etc.
Can pile objects, put in and pour out

Hand-Eye Coordination
Follows objects with her eyes
Reaches for objects
Looks at object when grasping it
Grasps objects offered to her
Looks for dropped object

When did pincer grasp, if any, disappear?

Was the grasping actively trained?

Hand-motor aids

Stereotypic Hand Movements
At what height does she hold her hands?
Arm movements
Hand movements
Finger movements
Rhythm Hand-to-mouth behavior, specify
Dominating hand
Any changes?
At what age did the stereotypic movements begin?

In what situations do they occur?

In what way do they cause problems?

Can they be subdued/made to cease, how?

Can they be used in a constructive manner, how?

Eating

Interest, degree of participation, own initiatives
Can finger-feed little pieces of fruit, bread, etc.
Can eat with spoon
Being fed by an adult
Needs minced/mashed/strained food
Can drink from a glass
Can take, hold, put down the glass by herself

Oral-pharyngeal motor activities
Chewing, how?
Swallowing
Biting off
Licking
Sucking (from a straw etc.)
Blowing
Peculiar mouth movements, when?

Refusal to eat, when, what?

Allergy to food

Need of liquid

Sense of taste
Sense of smell

Any aids for eating?

Toileting

Degree of independence/participation
Need of diapers
Any aids?

Dressing/undressing

Degree of independence/participation

Sleep

Need of sleep
Anything notable when falling asleep/waking up?
Sleeping mode
Sleeping position
Thumb-sucking
Are the stereotypic hand movements present during sleep?
Changes/variations in sleeping pattern

Needs and feelings

Hunger
How is the need expressed?
When is it expressed?
How is satisfaction of need expressed?

Thirst
How is the need expressed?
When is it expressed?
How is satisfaction of need expressed?

Going to the bathroom
How is the need expressed?
When is it expressed?
How is satisfaction of need expressed?

Sleep
How is the need expressed?
When is it expressed?
How is satisfaction of need expressed?

Need of company and social contacts
How is the need expressed?
When is it expressed?
How is satisfaction of need expressed?

Desire of certain activity
How is this desire expressed?
In which situations?

Joy
How is this expressed?
In which situations?
Non-situation-bound reactions

Unhappiness
How is this expressed?
In which situations?
Non-situation-bound reactions
Handling

Anger
How is this expressed?
In which situations?
Nonsituation-bound reactions
Handling her reaction

Fear
How is this expressed?
In which situations?
Nonsituation-bound reactions
Handling her reaction

Pain
How is this expressed?
In which situations?
Handling her reaction

Anticipation
How is this expressed?
In which situations?

Disappointment
How is this expressed?
In which situations?

Reactions to new situations
Unfamiliar environments
Strange people
New stimuli and events

Deviant behaviors
Extreme resistance to changes
Anxiety
Aggression/self-injury
Hyperactivity
Passivity
Extremely interested in details/fixations

Breath holding/hyperventilation/air swallowing
Grimaces
Peculiar eye movements
Teeth grinding
Withdrawal
In what situations do deviant behaviors occur?

In what way do they cause problems?

Can they be subdued/made to cease?

Any changes?

Variations/Fluctuations
In performance
In mood

In behavior
In degree of attention

Social Interaction and Communication

Contact
Difficulties
Radius
How to take/get best possible contact with the girl
Eye contact
Responsive smile
Reactions to bodily contact
Own initiatives to contact
Avoiding contact, how?
Discriminating familiar persons from strangers
Special favorites
Examples of special responses to certain people

Communication
Desire for communication
Ability of communication
Type of signals (words, gestures, signs, facial expressions, eyes, body language)
Special signs for yes — no, wants — does not want to
Are these signals spontaneous or learned?

Hearing and language
Response to sounds
Normal hearing
Radius
Locating ability
Auditory preferences
Ability to understand different sounds
Imitation of sounds
Interest in music

Comprehension of language
Responds appropriately to some words
Follows verbal directions
Likes to look at books, listen to stories
Can pronounce some words, which?
Other kinds of vocalization, type, consistence in use

Sight

Normal sight
Any visual problems, treatment?
Unusual reactions
Radius
Visual preferences

Smell and Taste, see "Eating"

Skin Sensitivity

Touching
Normal sensitivity
Preferences (texture, etc.)
Unusual reactions

Being touched
Responses to being touched
Locating ability
Unusual reactions

Temperature
Normal sensitivity
Unusual reactions

Pain
Normal sensitivity
Unusual reactions

Physical Symptoms

Gastrointestinal problems
Nausea, "saliva chewing," drooling, belching, vomiting
Air swallowing
Diarrhea, constipation, stomach complaints

Allergic symptoms
Eczema, spots, itching, edema, nasal catarrh

Hypersensitivity to light

Hypersensitivity to heat
In which situations do the symptoms occur?
In what way do they cause problems?
Handling/Treatment
Changes

Seizures
Type
Frequency
Changes and variations
Medical treatment

Self-awareness
Response to name
Response to mirror image
Response to photo of herself

Body awareness
Participation in ADL
Recognizes different parts of her body

Can point to/touch part of the body when asked to
Imitation

Cognitive skills
Comprehension of space
Comprehension of time
Comprehension of quality
Comprehension of picture
Comprehension of quantity
Comprehension of cause and effect

Activities
Type of spontaneous play/activity
Special interests
Favorite toys
Aversion to/fear of something

Learning
What does she learn
How does she learn
Degree and time of concentration

3 Questions Forming a Basis for Interviews with School Personnel

Girl's name_____ Age _____

School/preschool/day center

Class/group

Type of class/group

Number of students in class
Number of staff

Teacher
Type of education
Type of experience

Aides/assistants
Type of education
Type of experience

For how long has the girl been in this class/group?
For how long have the adults worked in this class/group?

Does the girl have a personal assistant?
Working time, hours a day
Working time, ratio school/home

Number of school days a week
Number of school hours a day
What is the cause if the girl does not have a full-time school week?

Should the school day be shorter/longer, why?

Ratio of time for one-to-one instruction/group instruction
Which activities are set aside for group versus one-to-one?
In what situations, and why, does the girl need one-to-one instruction?

Group interaction
To what degree does the girl participate?
Does she enjoy group interaction?
Special friends
Activities in/with other classes/groups

Schedule

What is given priority in training?
Is there an individual training program?

In what kinds of activities does the girl participate (swimming, horseback riding, physical training, waterplay, painting, cooking, field trips)?
Degree of participation
Own initiatives

Speech therapy
Number of hours a week
Training program
Experiences, positive/negative

Physical therapy
Number of hours a week, distribution
Training program
Who is carrying out the training?
Experiences, positive/negative

Pool baths
How often?
Special therapy
Water temperature
Reactions in water

Horseback riding
Aids

ADL (eating, toileting, dressing/undressing)
Ability
What has been better/worse?
What kind of training is offered?

Gross motor activities
Ability
What has been better/worse?
What kind of training is offered?

Hand motor activities
Ability
What has been better/worse

What kind of training is offered

Stereotypic hand movements
Do the stereotypies increase in some situations, if so, which?
In what way do they cause problems?
Can they be subdued/made to cease?
Variations/changes

Sensory ability
Unusual reactions
What has been better/worse?
What kind of training is offered?

Self-image (self-awareness, body awareness)
Ability
What has been better/worse?
What kind of training is offered?

Cognitive skills (time, space, cause-effect, quality, picture, quantity)
Ability
What has been better/worse?
What kind of training is offered?

Social interaction (ability to take and give contact)
Ability
What has been better/worse?
What kind of training is offered?

Communication
Ability and will
Type of signals
What has been better/worse?
What kind of training is offered?

Needs and feelings
Ability to interpret and express
What has been better/worse?
What kind of training is offered?

Will and initiative

Ability to express will and initiatives
What has been better/worse?
What kind of training is offered?

Examples of how the school settings are adapted to the girl's needs
(rooms, technical aids, communication methods)

Is the school and class chosen appropriate for the girl?
Difference between the girl and the rest of the group
Any needs of changing the group/class (how, why — students, adults, rooms, therapy)

What is most difficult with this student?
What is most important to change in her behavior/function?
What is most important to her?

Any wants for expert help concerning educational therapy?
Requirements for further education for personnel
Requirements for educational guidance
Requirements for psychological guidance
Requirements for support/advice/information

REFERENCES

GÖRANSSON, K., (1982). *Hur föståelsen av verkligheten utvecklas.* ALA/Handikappinstitutet: Stockholm, 1982.

HAGBERG, B. (1985). Rett's syndrome: Swedish approach to analysis of prevalence and cause. *Brain Dev.,* 7: 4.

HAGBERG, B., AICARDI, J., DIAS, K., RAMOS, O. (1983). A progressive syndrome of autism, dementia, ataxia, and loss of purposeful hand use in girls: Rett's syndrome: Report of 35 cases. *Ann. Neurol.,* 14: 471-479.

HAGBERG, B., GOUTIERES, F., HANEFELD F., RETT, A., WILSON, J., (1985). Rett syndrome: Criteria for inclusion and exclusion. *Brain Dev.,* 7: 372-373.

HAGBERG, B. WITT-ENGERSTRÖM I. (1985). Retts syndrom — en hjärnskada som ofta förväxlas med autism. *Ögonblick,* 4.

HAGBERG, B. WITT-ENGERSTRÖM I. (1985). Rett syndrome: A suggested staging system for describing impairment profile with increasing age towards adolescence. International Workshop on Rett syndrome, Baltimore, 1985.

KYLEN, G., (1974). Psykiskt utvecklingshämmades förstånd. *ALA - Rapport,* 162, Stockholm.

OLSSON B., RETT, A. (1985) Behavioral observations concerning differential diagnosis between the Rett syndrom and autism. *Brain Dev.,* 7: 281-289.

RETT, A. (1966). *Über ein cerebral-atrophisches Syndrom bei Hyperannomänie.* Hollinek: Wien, 1966.

WITT-ENGERSTRÖM, I. (1987). Tidig differentialdiagnostik mellan Retts Syndrom (R.S.) och Infantil Autism (I.A.). *BLF-nytt.,* 1.

INDEX